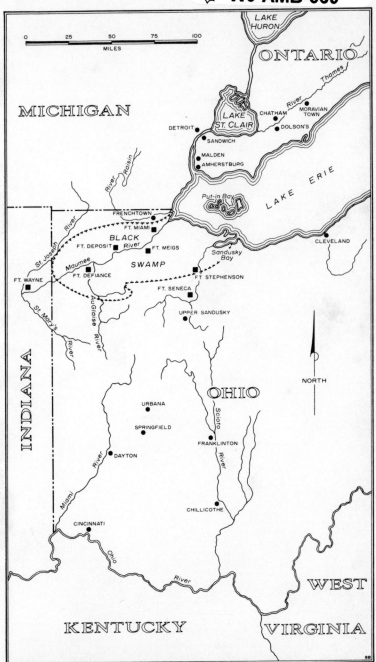

The Northwest Theater of War

Kentucky and the Second American Revolution

The War of 1812

JAMES WALLACE HAMMACK, JR.

THE UNIVERSITY PRESS OF KENTUCKY

To my Mother and Father

Research for The Kentucky Bicentennial Bookshelf
is assisted by a grant from the
National Endowment for the Humanities.
Views expressed in the Bookshelf do not
necessarily represent those of the Endowment.

ISBN: 0-8131-0216-2

Library of Congress Catalog Card Number: 75-41986

A statewide cooperative scholarly publishing agency
serving Berea College, Centre College of Kentucky,
Eastern Kentucky University, Georgetown College,
Kentucky Historical Society, Kentucky State University,
Morehead State University, Murray State University,
Northern Kentucky State College, Transylvania University,
University of Kentucky, University of Louisville, and
Western Kentucky University.

Editorial and Sales Offices: Lexington, Kentucky 40506

Contents

Acknowledgments

FEW BOOKS, IF ANY, are entirely the product of a single individual's efforts. Certainly this one is not. The assistance, encouragement, and criticism of several people were essential to the research upon which this book is based. My principal debt is to Professor Holman Hamilton, who spent many hours guiding and directing my research on the War of 1812. I am also grateful to Professors Carl B. Cone and James F. Hopkins, whose suggestions and knowledgeable comments influenced a number of my conclusions about Kentucky's role in the War of 1812.

For their aid in locating sources and furnishing guidance in the use of facilities I am indebted to librarians at many institutions. Because I applied to them more frequently for assistance, my debt is particularly great to the staffs of the University of Kentucky's Margaret I. King Library, the Kentucky Historical Society, and the Murray State University library. Many of the materials I found most useful were located at The Filson Club in Louisville, Kentucky, and for that reason I am especially appreciative of the generous assistance provided there and for permission from The Filson Club to use and quote from its archival collections.

Finally I must acknowledge that without the encouragement of my wife Charlotte, who endured many impositions and generously assumed a disproportionate share of family responsibilities for a long time, the writing of this book could not have taken place.

Introduction

THE WAR OF 1812 had its origins in Anglo-American controversies over neutral rights during a period when the world's greatest powers, Great Britain and France, were locked in mortal combat. But for the post-Revolutionary War generation of young Kentuckians, the War of 1812 seemed as much a war for American independence as was the Revolution itself. Upon learning, in June 1812, that the United States had declared war against Great Britain, the Lexington *Reporter* proclaimed: "The dreadful, deadly chord [*sic*] which anchored us along side of death and destruction is once more cut, and we are again afloat on the sea of liberty." Echoing that sentiment in their official pronouncement of support for the war, members of the Kentucky General Assembly resolved that the British government's "pertinacious adherence to Claims which no Nation ought to submit to" had left the United States no option but armed resistance.

That Kentuckians were prepared to offer far more in support of the American war effort than paper resolutions and wordy editorials was immediately evident. So great was the rush to the colors by eager volunteers following the declaration of war that many were turned away for lack of arms and powder with which to equip them. Few who sought service against the British and their Indian allies would be disappointed for long, however. Before the conflict ended in early 1815, an astonishingly high percentage of eligible Kentucky males were enrolled for varying periods of military service either as regulars, volunteers, or militia.

Nor were those Kentuckians who donned the uniform of their state or nation merely parade-ground soldiers. Thomas Jefferson's prediction that the conquest of Canada would be simply "a matter of marching," and Henry Clay's assurances that the Kentucky militia alone would suffice to capture Quebec, proved equally fatuous. From the outset, Kentucky's citizen-soldiers found themselves involved in some of the heaviest fighting of the war. The fortitude with which they bore both defeat and victory soon established for the state an enduring reputation for patriotic ardor and military valor in the national interest. Within a year of the outbreak of war in 1812, Kentucky's unstinting exertions were being pointed to by eastern politicians and journalists as an example for the remainder of the Union to emulate.

It is understandable that succeeding generations of historians, intrigued by the heroism and perseverance attributed to Kentucky's fighting men, have invariably tended to leave the state scene behind in their writings on the War of 1812 and follow Kentucky's armies into the field. As a result, much is known of Kentuckians' deeds on the battlefield. The names of such state heroes as Zachary Taylor, George Croghan, William Whitley, Richard M. Johnson, and Isaac Shelby are indelibly inscribed in the annals of Kentucky's past. The battle cry "Remember the Raisin!" continues to ring through the pages of Kentucky history as loudly as it once rang through the swamps and forests of the Old Northwest. Vividly portrayed, too, in writings on the War of 1812 are the death throes of the wounded Kentucky prisoners slaughtered by drunken Indians after being defeated at the River Raisin, the anguished torment of Kentuckians forced by their Indian captors to run the gauntlet following "Dudley's Defeat" opposite Fort Meigs, and the thundering charge of Richard M. Johnson's mounted volunteers as they broke the British lines in the Battle of the Thames.

But the individual and collective stories of heroism and infamy, of suffering and courage, which make up the record of Kentucky campaigns against the enemy are not the full story of the state's participation in the War of 1812. Any impression that enthusiasm and support for the war remained at a consistently high level in Kentucky throughout the conflict is a mistaken one. Kentuckians would have been less than human had their ardor for war been unaffected by the military reverses inflicted upon their friends and kinsmen or had they failed to react to political, diplomatic, and military developments elsewhere in the nation. Similarly, Kentucky's failures and successes in the campaigns of 1812–1815 can never be fully explained by accounts of mistaken tactics or unusual bravery on the battlefield. To a large extent, the foundations both for defeat and victory were laid by changing attitudes and conditions within the state, and by preparations and plans made before any single contingent of troops marched beyond the state's borders. It is primarily the story of those internal and external conditions which shaped Kentucky's military record in the War of 1812 that will be told in this volume.

1

THE CALL TO BATTLE

WHEN THE NEWS reached Kentucky on July 15, 1803, that Great Britain and France were again at war after less than two years of peace, it caused little excitement. In the Frankfort *Palladium*, the editor, William Hunter, termed the resumption of war in Europe a "highly interesting" development. It would, he predicted, "necessarily have some effect on the commerce and foreign relations of the United States." But few in Kentucky suspected that the effect would be so great as to lead the United States to declare war on Great Britain nine years later.

Even the events of 1804 to 1806 caused relatively little alarm in Kentucky, although it was during those years that the foundations for war between Great Britain and her former colonies were laid. The accession of William Pitt to power in England in April 1804 marked the beginning of a new and uncompromising British attitude toward neutrals that soon led to a crisis in Anglo-American relations. Almost immediately after Pitt took office the number of alleged British subjects impressed by British naval officers from the crews of American merchant vessels on the high seas increased sharply.

But the heaviest blows to American commercial interests resulted from Pitt's determination to curtail trade between neutral nations and England's enemies. In the spring of 1805, a British court declared illegal the lucrative American practice of converting goods from the French West Indies into "neutral" goods by taking them to United States ports before shipping them on to France. On the oceans British captains gleefully set about enforcing the court decision. And soon afterward two British warships, the *Cambrian* and the *Leander*, boldly took up regular station at New York, where they frequently held as many as "a dozen, and sometimes a couple of dozen" American ships waiting within sight of the port to be searched.

The rising toll of impressments and of condemnations of American ships and cargoes soon reached such proportions that mariners and shippers from Maine to Virginia began voicing angry protests against British obstructions to American neutral commerce. Amidst much talk of war, mass meetings were held at seaports along the Atlantic in September and October 1805 to demand protection for American ships and seamen against British depredations.

When word of Britain's maritime practices reached the West some Kentuckians, quickly aroused by any hint of foreign infringements upon American rights of self-government, joined in the outcry. "Are we to Suffer the English Nation to do as they please with our Ships and Country Men?" Colonel George Thompson angrily inquired in a letter to Kentuckian John Breckinridge, President Thomas Jefferson's attorney general. "I had rather have the Indians to reign over me than the British government," the irate Mercer County planter exclaimed. The rising, young, Lexington lawyer Henry Clay was also moved to suggest, "Perhaps this is a fortunate moment to repel European aggression, and to evince to the world that Americans appreciate their rights in such a way as will induce them, when violated, to engage in War with alacrity and effect."

For the moment, however, such protests as were heard from Kentucky remained isolated, individual expressions of sentiment. In the midst of the rising clamor in the port cities of the United States, the Kentucky General Assembly declared its hope that the remoteness of the struggle in Europe would allow the United States to "continue safe from the contagion" of the spreading European war. Kentucky's legislators, far from sympathizing with demands for bellicose action against Great Britain, resolved that Europe's problems should teach Americans to appreciate their happy state "by the contrast they afford with the peace and tranquility which surrounds us." And in Congress most of Kentucky's congressional delegation joined in arguing that restrictions imposed by belligerent nations upon neutral trade were primarily a private problem of American shippers rather than a matter of national concern.

It was the crashing broadsides fired by the British warship *Leopard* into the United States frigate *Chesapeake* on June 22, 1807, that first raised Anglo-American maritime problems to a level of general concern in Kentucky. The *Chesapeake* was bound for the Mediterranean, when it stood out to sea from Hampton Roads, Virginia. Although a British squadron had for some time been lying in wait for a handful of French warships huddled together in the Virginia port, none of the officers of the *Chesapeake* anticipated trouble from the navy of a nation with which the United States was at peace. The *Chesapeake* was thus unprepared for action when it was hailed by the *Leopard* shortly after passing the limit of national waters. An unprecedented demand that alleged British deserters among the crew of the American naval vessel be surrendered created consternation aboard the *Chesapeake.* Quite properly, Commodore James Barron refused to allow his ship to be searched by a British boarding party. Upon receiving his refusal, the *Leopard* opened fire at point blank range. Within ten minutes, Barron, unable to bring his own dismounted guns into action, was forced to strike his flag and permit the removal of four men from his vessel. In the littered wreckage on the shot-torn deck of the *Chesapeake* three Americans lay dead and eighteen wounded.

Kentuckians greeted news of the *Chesapeake* affair with an almost universal demand for retaliation. There was much talk of both embargo and war. But the *Kentucky Gazette* best expressed the mood of the moment when it declared, "The tocsin is now sounded!" In towns and counties across the state militia units paraded and Kentucky citizens gathered to shout their protests against Britain's flagrant disregard for the sovereignty and dignity of the United States. In Scott and Harrison counties resolutions were adopted recommending that all trade and diplomatic relations with Great Britain be severed. At Nicholasville and Paris, and at meetings in Mercer, Boone, and Jessamine counties, aroused Kentuckians pledged their "lives and fortunes" in support of whatever retaliatory measures the Jefferson administration adopted. Louisvillians thronged to the Jefferson County courthouse to decry the "wanton and unprovoked outrage" on the national flag and to insist that "nothing less than a propitiation as bloody as the outrage itself can atone for the insult." Elsewhere, the commanders of Kentucky's militia regiments declared the *Leopard*'s attack on the *Chesapeake* an act of war. At Georgetown and at Traveller's Hall in Lexington regimental officers met to pledge their last drop of blood in defense of American liberties. They preferred, they proclaimed, that their "bones should bleach on the plains of Canada and the distant shores of Nova Scotia," before British infringements upon American rights should pass "without that chastisement which they deserve."

The most important effect of the *Chesapeake* affair upon Kentucky was the change that it wrought in Kentuckians' attitudes toward Britain's maritime practices. Never, after 1807, would influential Kentucky political leaders argue that British restrictions upon American commerce were a matter of private rather than public concern. The attack on the *Chesapeake* became widely accepted in Kentucky as positive proof that Britain's Orders in Council, adopted in 1806 and early 1807 for the purpose of preventing contraband goods from reaching the Continent in neutral ships, were aimed less at France than at the United States. Kentucky editors and political leaders charged that Britain's ministers, motivated by jealousy of American commercial prosperity and hostility to republican institutions everywhere, were using the excuse of war in Europe to regulate American trade for England's benefit. The British government's ultimate goal, they claimed, was to make the United States economically dependent upon, and thus politically subservient to, Great Britain.

This interpretation of the Anglo-American maritime controversy was consistently adhered to both by the Republican press and legislature in Kentucky and by most of the state's representatives in Congress from 1807 until war was declared in 1812. More than any other factor, it accounted for the Kentucky position on relations between the United States and Great Britain during that period. Every new effort by Britain to strengthen its blockade of France after 1807 served to reinforce in Kentucky the conviction that resistance to British encroachments upon American rights, even to the point of war, was mandatory in the name of national independence. That Napoleon Bonaparte, through his Berlin and Milan decrees, was attempting to use French control of the European continent similarly to restrict neutral trade with Great Britain did little to alter hostility in Kentucky toward England. Kentuckians argued that, unlike Great Britain, France had no territorial ambitions in North America and no ulterior designs upon American independence.

The fires of war fever that raged through Kentucky in the wake of the *Chesapeake* affair were banked, but were not extinguished, by President Jefferson's decision to avoid an armed conflict with Great Britain if at all possi-

5

ble. Kentuckians, in the years preceding the War of 1812, were overwhelmingly Jeffersonian Republican in their politics. The Federalist party was widely despised as a party of privileged, pro-British, anti-western interest groups; and the tiny minority of Federalist partisans within the state exerted almost no influence in Kentucky political affairs. Thus when Jefferson, in late 1807, sought to coerce Britain and France into removing their restrictions on neutral commerce by requesting an embargo on all American trade with foreign nations, most Kentuckians were prepared faithfully to follow their political idol's lead.

From December 1807 until the eve of the War of 1812, the United States experimented with several forms of economic coercion as substitutes for war. By March 1809, shortly before Jefferson retired from office to be succeeded by James Madison, it had become apparent that the effects of the Embargo Act upon American shippers and exporters were so disastrous that the measure could not be longer sustained. A modification was passed in the form of the Non-Intercourse Act, which permitted trade with all nations except Britain, France, and their allies. Even this did not satisfy the growing number of critics of economic coercion, and in May 1810 still another change in American foreign policy was proposed by the House Foreign Relations Committee. To the embarrassment of committee chairman Nathaniel Macon of North Carolina, who opposed the policy changes recommended by the Foreign Relations Committee, the legislation enacted by Congress came to be known by his name. Macon's Bill #2 can more correctly be termed a measure of economic enticement than economic coercion. In contrast to the Non-Intercourse Act it freed Americans to trade with all nations, including Britain and France. But it provided that if either of the belligerent nations removed its restrictions on United States commerce, non-intercourse would be restored against the other belligerent power.

Through all of these changes in American foreign policy, Kentuckians continued to insist upon the necessity of resisting British infringements upon the sovereignty of the United States. But as each succeeding measure passed by Congress weakened the original Jeffersonian concept of economic coercion, confidence in congressional management of foreign affairs waned in the state. From the outset, Macon's Bill #2 was widely considered by Kentuckians to be a shamefully weak, faltering response to overt aggressions on American rights. One member of the state General Assembly, upon reading the debates in Congress over the proposed bill, exclaimed: "Great God, that my country should be thus scandalized to the world!—It makes my face burn with shame barely to read the speeches made in *the Congress of America.*" During the same period Thomas Todd of Danville, an associate justice of the Supreme Court, found the "disorder and confusion" in Congress "truly disgusting." It was exceeded, he wrote, "in no Legislative body within his knowledge save that of the Ohio State, or a mob."

Final enactment of Macon's Bill #2 almost totally discredited the Eleventh Congress in Kentucky as an effective governing body. Throughout the state Humphrey Marshall's recently established Federalist newspaper, the *American Republic,* stood nearly alone in applauding the latest turn in American foreign policy. The more widely read *Kentucky Gazette,* together with other Republican newspapers, loudly bemoaned the retreat from firm resistance by a Congress which seemed "interposed like a *mountain of ice,* between the American people and their enemies." And at Fourth of July celebrations in Kentucky in 1810 patriotic citizens lifted their mugs and demanded from Congress "More unanimity, more energetic measures, and fewer long-winded speeches."

At least one impatient advocate of war recognized, however, that few Kentuckians had by 1810 entirely abandoned hopes that American rights could be safeguarded without resorting to war. "Annually (the 4th July) we are seized by a *war fever,*" he wrote in disgust following the 1810 celebrations. "Every pigmy becomes a Goliath. We make a few blustering, bombastic speeches; pass a string of *pointed* resolutions; look big; strut about in all the majesty of independence; toast the French and English to the devil; get a little fuddled; and sleep off the *fever* the following night. . . . I think we have rather too much wind for our ballast."

The last vestiges of hope that Britain would abandon impressment and that a change in Britain's Orders in Council could be brought about by economic coercion disappeared rapidly, however. Two events in 1811 signaled an end to support for economic coercion in Kentucky and led to a widespread demand for immediate war. The first stemmed from Napoleon Bonaparte's apparent acquiescence in the proposition offered by Macon's Bill #2. In August 1810 Napoleon's foreign minister, the Duc de Cadore, notified the Madison administration that restrictions on American commerce under the Berlin and Milan decrees would be repealed. In Lexington, William Worsley, editor of the *Reporter*, exulted that the indecisive, lame-duck Eleventh Congress would have little choice but to defy the British Orders in Council by reviving non-intercourse against Great Britain alone. Worsley was right. Although Congress debated at length, the necessary legislation to enforce non-intercourse against England was finally passed on February 28, 1811.

To Kentuckians, this seemed the final test for economic coercion as an effective form of resistance to British infringements on American maritime rights. If Britain failed to yield to the pressure of non-intercourse while American trade with France continued, the only alternatives in the opinion of Kentucky statesmen were war or submission. Britain's reply to the restoration of non-intercourse was extremely slow in coming, however, and during the spring and summer of 1811 predictions of inevitable war multiplied rapidly in Kentucky. Kentuckians were not surprised, therefore, when in August

Britain's official refusal to comply with American demands was received by Madison. Their response to the news was a united and unequivocal demand for war.

When the Twelfth Congress convened in Washington three months later Kentucky's delegates, with a single exception, could already be numbered among the faction later known as War Hawks. Convinced that the time had come to fight for American rights, they welcomed the message sent to Congress on November 5 by Madison in which he spoke bluntly of Britain's "hostile inflexibility in trampling on rights which no independent nation can relinquish." Enthusiastically they applauded the president's request that Congress put the United States "into an armor and attitude demanded by the crisis, and corresponding with the national spirit and expectations."

Henry Clay, the newly elected Speaker of the House of Representatives, immediately set about organizing that body for war by appointing advocates of armed resistance to the more important House committees. In his efforts to move Congress toward a declaration of war Clay was ably assisted by other members of the Kentucky delegation. Most prominent among these were Joseph Desha of Mason County and Richard M. Johnson of Scott County. Desha, who had fought in the Indian wars in the Northwest at the age of fifteen and who had served nine consecutive terms in the state legislature before being elected to Congress, became a principal figure on the House Foreign Relations Committee. A member of Congress since 1807, Johnson was also an experienced legislator and a man of varied talents. His octoroon mistress was reputed to be "the most beautiful girl in the West," and he was the author of a pamphlet on light cavalry tactics which Napoleon had reportedly read and complimented. Short of stature, red-haired and fiery-tempered, Johnson was, next to Clay, Kentucky's most powerful orator in the House. In the Twelfth Congress all of his oratorical abilities were directed toward war against Great Britain. Repeatedly, he lashed out at those who

9

were reluctant to take up arms in defense of American sovereignty. "[Britain's] infernal system has driven us to the brink of a second revolution, as important as the first," he proclaimed in thundering tones. "We must now oppose the farther encroachments of Great Britain by war, or formally annul the Declaration of our Independence, and acknowledge ourselves her devoted colonies."

By fall of 1811 there were few in Kentucky who disagreed with Johnson's contention that only through war could the United States force Britain's government "to treat us as an independent people." To Humphrey Marshall, the acknowledged leader of Kentucky Federalists, Madison's "great war speech" of November 5 had the sound of "an empty tub." But the Lexington *Reporter* and the Republican-dominated General Assembly heartily approved Madison's apparent determination to bring an end to the congressional policy of "protracted moderation" in relations with Great Britain. Confidently expecting a presidential request for a declaration of war in the near future, their only anxiety was whether the Twelfth Congress would acquiesce in Madison's demand or would instead follow the humiliating example set by the preceding Congress.

While Britain's refusal to relinquish the Orders in Council caused Kentuckians to believe that war was necessary, a second event later that same year on the American northwest frontier caused them to believe that an immediate declaration of war was imperative. By the summer of 1811 the gifted Shawnee leader, Tecumseh, and his half-brother, the Prophet, had succeeded in uniting a number of Indian tribes in the Northwest in opposition to further territorial encroachments by Americans. These tribes were England's natural allies in western America and were known to be supplied from British posts in Canada. In late August the *Kentucky Gazette* announced that William Henry Harrison, governor of Indiana Territory, was preparing to lead an armed expedition to the Prophet's settlement on Tippecanoe

Creek in the Wabash River region of Indiana Territory. Behind a show of force, Harrison hoped to awe the Prophet into recognizing the validity of a land cession treaty recently concluded with tribes not aligned with Tecumseh's confederation. But on the night of November 7, 1811, the Prophet directed his followers in a fierce, bloodily repulsed night attack on Harrison's encampment.

Coming so close upon the heels of Britain's adamant refusal to set aside restrictions on United States trade with Europe, the Battle of Tippecanoe convinced Kentuckians that the British government had anticipated an American declaration of war by opening hostilities upon the western frontier. "It is not to be believed that these Savages would contend, single handed, with the force of the United States, which they well know could crush them at a blow," Governor Charles Scott declared. "The hand of British intrigue is not difficult to be perceived in this thing." Echoing these sentiments, the editor of the Lexington *Reporter* wrote: "You may as well call the revolutionary war, a Hessian war because the Hessians were hired by the British, as to term this an Indian war."

The experiment in economic coercion had failed. President Madison had already requested Congress to take steps preparatory to a declaration of war. Surely, Kentucky advocates of war argued, there could be no reason consistent with either prudence or national honor for further delay. For, as the *Kentucky Gazette* declared upon receiving reports from Tippecanoe, "War we now have!"

Kentuckians' hopes for an immediate declaration of war were, however, doomed to frustration. Although Congress, as early as December 1811, accepted a report from the House Foreign Relations Committee recommending an increase in the size of the regular army, a levy of 50,000 volunteers, the arming of merchant vessels, and the fitting out of all repairable warships not in service, months of lengthy debate and deliberate preparations for hostilities lay ahead. Meanwhile, impatience with the dilatory behavior of the Twelfth Congress mounted steadily in Kentucky. The suspicion arose that Congress would in the end permit itself to be duped into peace by seizing upon any minor British concession as an excuse to avoid war. As this suspicion gained strength, demands for an immediate declaration of war grew louder and more urgent.

By early February 1812, banqueters at a public dinner in Lexington were expressing their dissatisfaction in a toast to "The Present Congress—May it end the war of words and bring the decision of our differences with foreign powers to the mouth of the cannon." Even the prospect of heavier taxes in the event of war did not deter Kentucky War Hawks from their goal. As mid-March approached and Congress continued its lengthy and hesitant debates over the sensitive question of imposing new taxes to finance the proposed war, the editor of the Lexington *Reporter* could restrain his impatience no longer. In a slashing editorial attack upon the national legislature, Worsley declared that he had refrained from criticizing Congress "whilst they were disposed to do something, however slow; when they were in the *right road*, we were willing to let them continue on in their own *snail's pace* without interruption." But he could no longer excuse "pretended fears" that Americans would not defend their independence if it meant increased taxes. "We have never heard an objection to the paying of taxes," the Kentucky editor asserted. "If any taxes are unequal and oppressive this year, alter them the next. *But no submission to Britain.* This is the constant language we have heard."

In April it appeared, momentarily, that an end to the period of waiting was at hand. In the House of Representatives a bill establishing a sixty-day embargo on American shipping was passed for the purpose of clearing American vessels from the ocean before a declaration of war was adopted. Reports of the House action in the Lexington *Reporter* were headlined "HIGHLY IMPORTANT—The die is cast!" War, the *Reporter* jubilantly declared, was now inevitable. But once more, there was disappointment. In the Senate, the embargo period was extended to ninety days, and Kentuckians were again left to wonder whether Congress really intended war.

Not until late June were all doubts of congressional intentions dispelled in Kentucky. On June 1, Kentuckians learned ten days later, President Madison had formally requested Congress to declare war against Great Britain. With the single exception of Senator John Pope, all of Kentucky's representatives in Congress rejoiced at the presidential request. Kentucky members of the House of Representatives unanimously approved when, on June 4, that body voted 79–49 for war. But when the Senate, on June 17, finally concurred with the decision of the lower house by a vote of 19–13, Pope stood with the opposition.

Together with Henry Clay and Felix Grundy, John Pope had been one of the dominant figures in the Kentucky General Assembly before his election to the United States Senate in 1806. Known to friends and foes alike as "One-arm Pope," a condition resulting from a boyhood accident, the Republican senator considered himself a straight party man. His early senatorial career lent credence to that description, and in early 1808 Pope unblushingly claimed that "except [John] Breckinridge no man from the West ever had more popularity in Congress" than himself. But Pope's vote against war in 1812 spelled ruin for his immediate political ambitions. His explanation that war should have been declared against France as well as Britain and his claim that he would have supported a declaration of war against both belligerents went unheeded in the state. So great was the enthusiasm for war in Kentucky in 1812, that it would be years before the errant senator regained a measure of his former popularity.

All that was now required to make the declaration of war official was Madison's signature. And on June 18 the president inscribed his name on the historic document. The excitement touched off in Kentucky by this action approached pandemonium. Observers reported that "the news of war was hailed as a second decree of Independence." Throughout the state, towns and villages were "illuminated" on the occasion, as cheering crowds gathered to pledge their support for the war effort. At Lexington, Frankfort, and in numerous other communities, public celebrations, accompanied by the incessant firing of cannons and muskets, lasted late into the evening. The frenzied citizens of the state, the *Kentucky Gazette* exclaimed, appeared ready to hurl themselves en masse upon the British and their Indian allies.

Nor did the passions unleashed by the news of war die quickly. Fourth of July celebrations in Kentucky were more riotous than usual in 1812. Orators reached new heights of eloquence in their efforts to revive the "spirit of '76," and toasts vowing death and destruction to the enemies of American independence were drunk with unprecedented fervor. In late July when Henry Clay returned home from Washington, public sentiment was still so aroused that Clay professed to "have almost been alarmed at the ardor which has been displayed, knowing how prone human nature is to extremes." For John Pope homecoming must have been an unpleasant ordeal. In the press and in the streets, Pope's record in the Twelfth Congress was assailed as anti-Republican and his vote against war was bitterly reviled. In more than one Kentucky community, effigies of the unfortunate senator were burned over roaring bonfires.

The unrestrained ardor with which Kentuckians greeted news of the declaration of war in 1812 was fostered by a variety of emotions and aspirations. In part it was a product of traditional western Anglophobia, heightened by recent clashes with the British and their Indian allies over commercial rights and territorial expansion. Romanticized expectations of military glory also contributed to the enthusiasm of many individual War Hawks. To a greater extent, Kentuckians' enthusiasm for war was produced by an exuberant nationalism, which demanded that the newly independent United States be accorded every measure of respect due a sovereign nation.

But the enthusiasm with which the outbreak of war was celebrated in Kentucky was obviously intensified by feelings of relief that the nation's leaders, after years of indecision and doubt, had finally foresworn further submission to British dictates. The Lexington *Reporter* pointedly expressed the sense of relieved elation felt by many Kentuckians, when it exulted that Congress had at last been "*driven, goaded, dragged, forced, kicked,* by the *unaccountable* madness, folly and desperation of the British government" into an unalterable policy of resistance to infringements on American rights.

2

THE MOST
PATRIOTIC PEOPLE

FOR THE YOUNG United States war against Great Britain
was a daring and hazardous enterprise. Great Britain, in
the early nineteenth century, was preeminent on the
oceans and in the colonial world. In Europe Britain's
power was rivaled only by that of France. So long as the
Napoleonic wars lasted, it could be predicted with cer-
tainty that the principal weight of England's military
might would be directed against France and her allies.
But if England succeeded in defeating Napoleon in
Europe, the United States would be left to stand alone
against the world's mightiest nation.

In contrast to England's great strength, the Federal
Union at the time war was declared was comprised of
only seventeen states. Despite territorial claims that
stretched westward toward the Pacific Northwest, Kentucky, Tennessee, and Ohio were the only American
states lying west of the Appalachian Mountains. Louisiana would be admitted to the Union before the end of
1812, but the remainder of the vast American West was
divided into the territories of Missouri, Mississippi, Indiana, Illinois, and Michigan. With few exceptions, these
territories were sparsely settled and in a frontier stage of
development.

Among the western states and territories Kentucky was
by far the most populous and most economically ad-

vanced. Kentucky's population of well over 400,000 in 1812 represented more than a third of the people in the entire trans-Appalachian West. In addition to an extensive, diversified agricultural economy, the Bluegrass region of the state boasted a growing number of budding manufacturing enterprises. Lexington, in the heart of the Bluegrass, was the largest city west of Pittsburgh and was generally regarded as the "principal seat of wealth and refinement" in the western country. As marks of Lexington's growing "refinement," the city's officials had long ago passed laws prohibiting such dangerous frontier practices as the building of wooden chimneys, the lighting of fires with rifles, the racing of horses in streets, and the keeping of pet panthers. Further signs of an advancing cultural life approaching that of many eastern cities could be seen in Transylvania College, in Lexington's two newspapers, its public library, its several jockey clubs, and in a variety of schools offering lessons in genteel pastimes such as fencing, French, and dancing.

As a result of its larger population and more well-rounded economy, Kentucky, on the eve of the War of 1812, held a place of acknowledged leadership in western affairs. According to one contemporary observer, Kentucky was the "focus of military and political movement" in the trans-Appalachian West. Another observer, after traveling through the Ohio and Mississippi River valleys, declared a few years later: "From the Allegany hills to the Rocky Mountains, the character of this state [Kentucky] has a certain preponderance. Her modes of thinking and action dictate the fashion to the rest." With war approaching, it was inevitable that Kentucky would be expected to carry much of the burden of military operations in the West. The fervor with which Kentuckians celebrated the declaration of war was indicative of the confidence with which they were prepared to assume large responsibilities in the fighting that lay ahead.

In their enthusiasm for war, however, many Kentuckians either ignored or deprecated the perils of the trial which the nation faced. That the perils would be numerous was almost unavoidable. For the United States was woefully ill prepared for war in June of 1812. The Navy Department had only twenty vessels at its disposal when war began and was therefore incapable of either controlling the lakes on the Canadian border or of protecting the seacoast. The ten existing regiments of the army were poorly equipped, their ranks were only half filled, and their component units were posted at garrisons scattered all across the country. In the Northwest Territory where Britain's Indian allies were already in arms, the army's lines were stretched so thin that the frontiers were nearly defenseless.

Although Congress had authorized an additional thirteen regiments of regulars and a separate force of 50,000 one-year volunteers, enlistments were dishearteningly slow. By the end of June the regular army was still no more than one-third its total authorized strength of 35,600 men. Recruiting for the volunteer army had proceeded even more slowly. In the field a force of 1,800 men under the reluctant command of sixty-year-old William Hull had been ordered to Detroit prior to the commencement of the war. But Hull's army was nearly three weeks from its destination when war was declared.

Worse still, the declaration of war failed to heal the divisions that had plagued congressional direction of foreign affairs since 1807. The ruinous effects of the Embargo Act upon American shipping interests had caused many New England Federalists bitterly to oppose any disruption of normal relations with Britain. Angered by the declaration of war and fearful of its economic consequences, they continued to hamper congressional preparations for the conflict. At the same time, Republican members were also deeply divided over issues that affected voters' pocketbooks.

At the instigation of Republican War Hawks, Congress had earlier adopted resolutions proposing new taxes in the event of war. But those resolutions had not actually been enacted into law. When, having declared war, it became incumbent upon Congress to consider enactment of the proposed funding program, the House of Representatives refused. Members who had loudly demanded war a few days earlier grew hesitant when confronted with the onerous duty of imposing taxes upon the public. Kentucky's representatives were among those who breathed a sigh of relief upon hearing a motion to postpone the passage of war taxes until the next session of Congress. Despite the imminence of war, Richard M. Johnson was in the forefront of the movement for postponement. The honor of every man in the House, he insisted, was pledged to support the war. With great fervor Johnson solemnly declared that he decidedly favored ample taxes to fund the nation's military effort. But, he rather lamely concluded, he would postpone the tax question solely from a desire to get home after eight months in Washington. When Congress did agree to adjourn without providing the necessary financial means with which to wage war, not a single Kentucky vote was cast against postponement of the tax question.

In their disregard for the fundamental importance of providing monetary means to carry on the war, Kentucky congressmen were motivated by the same reckless impatience for action that afflicted their constituents. The thoughts of politicians and ordinary citizens alike turned solely upon their urgent desire to carry the fight to the enemy. Neither had time for the mundane details of organizing the American war effort. The last tap of the gavel signaling adjournment had scarcely ceased echoing through the halls of Congress, before Kentucky's members were on their way home to share the dangers and hardships of service in the war they had helped bring about.

By October 1812, six of the Kentucky congressional delegation were in uniform. Samuel Hopkins returned from Washington to resume his duties as major general of the Kentucky militia. During the war he campaigned actively against the Indians along the exposed Illinois and Indiana frontiers. Richard M. Johnson raised a regiment of mounted volunteers and led them to lasting renown at the Battle of the Thames in Upper Canada. John Simpson and William P. Duvall both served as captains in the northwestern campaigns of 1812 and 1813. Two other Kentucky congressmen, Samuel McKee and Thomas Montgomery, shouldered muskets and marched off to war as privates. Although Henry Clay remained at his post as Speaker of the House, his role as chief of the congressional War Hawks and later as one of the American peacemakers at Ghent has linked his name more closely to the War of 1812 than that of perhaps any other American except Andrew Jackson.

During the latter half of 1812 Kentuckians of every age and station in life were quick to emulate the example set by the state's political elite. The pledges of support for the American war effort that had poured from every county in the state in June and July were soon redeemed by offers to serve in the contemplated offensive against Canada. Businessmen closed their ledgers, laborers laid aside their tools, and farmers left their fields in response to the first calls for volunteers. In Lexington, Thomas Smith, editor of the *Kentucky Gazette* and a noted advocate of war, left his desk a few weeks after printing the news that war had been declared and rode off to join the fighting. John Adair, a veteran of the American Revolution and a former United States senator, wrote directly to the governor volunteering his services during the conflict. Himself a future governor, Adair was destined to play an important part in both the Battle of the Thames and the Battle of New Orleans.

By the end of the year 1812 nearly two and a half regiments of Kentucky troops had been enlisted into the regular army of the United States for a period of "five years or the duration of the war." These included the bulk of the Seventh United States Infantry Regiment, all of the Seventeenth, and half of the Nineteenth. None of these units quite attained the standard regimental strength of 1,068 officers and men established by Congress in an act of June 26, 1812. But the Seventh and the Seventeenth mustered 907 and 979 officers and men respectively. And the smaller Nineteenth Regiment apparently included about 350 Kentuckians and an equal number of Ohioans. During this same period a far larger number of Kentuckians elected to serve in militia or in volunteer units. Altogether, Kentucky in 1812 provided a total of 11,114 regulars, militia, and volunteers for the war.

The readiness with which Kentuckians answered the call to arms after the declaration of war soon caught the admiring attention of much of the rest of the nation. A Boston merchant traveling through the state in 1813 wrote of Kentuckians, "they are the most patriotic people I have ever seen or heard of." He was particularly astonished at the number of forty- and fifty-year-old men, often men of wealth and prominence, who had risked their "lives and fortunes" as volunteers in the war. "These things to a New-Englandman look like madness," he wrote, "[but] here it is considered glorious, as it really is." Others, too, were soon expressing a similar admiration for the manner in which Kentuckians fulfilled their pledges to support the second American war against Great Britain. The war had not progressed far before eastern journals like the Boston *Patriot,* the Baltimore *American,* and New York's Albany *Argus* began pointing to Kentucky patriotism as an example for other states to emulate.

The growing reputation that Kentucky early acquired for patriotism and valor was based not only upon the alacrity with which citizens of the state flocked to the colors, but also upon the reckless daring displayed by a host of individual Kentuckians in the initial campaigns of the war. The degree to which the United States depended upon poorly trained militia forces in the War of 1812 placed an unusually high premium upon individual initiative and daring on the field of battle. And few states emerged from the contest with as many military heroes as Kentucky. Even before war was declared, two of the Kentucky dead at Tippecanoe had been widely honored as gallant victims of British aggression. In late 1811 the Kentucky General Assembly went into official mourning for Colonel Abraham Owen, who had fallen at the side of William Henry Harrison while assisting to form a line of defense against the Prophet's warriors. At a later date Owen's name would be given to a county in the state. Kentucky's legislators had also resolved to wear black crepe armbands in memory of Colonel Joseph Hamilton Daviess, who had been fatally wounded in a futile charge against the Indians at Tippecanoe. Better known than Owen, Daviess would have counties in at least four western states named in his honor.

To a degree, however, the patriotic zeal that Kentuckians so abundantly displayed in the early months of the war was symptomatic of their basic failure to understand the strengths and weaknesses of either the United States or Great Britain. Their ardor for military service, as well as their lack of concern over Congress's failure to make adequate preparations for hostilities against a major power, were due in large part to unrealistic, preconceived expectations of the course the war would follow. Those expectations made it appear that extensive preparations for war were not crucial to victory. The same expectations also had a direct effect upon the role that Kentucky played in the war and upon the decline of war spirit in the state after 1812.

The first assumption upon which Kentuckians based their hopes for victory in the War of 1812 was that Britain's involvement in the war in Europe would make it necessary for British military planners to adopt an exclusively defensive strategy in Canada. It was widely assumed that so long as the European war lasted, Britain's offensive efforts against the United States would be limited to naval operations against American shipping and seaports. To counter this, the United States was expected to release swarms of privateers to disrupt British commerce and communications on the ocean, while American land forces assaulted Canada. The conquest of British Canada, many Kentuckians believed, would force Great Britain to sue for peace on American terms. At the same time, it would pacify the Indians in the Northwest by eliminating their major source of arms and supplies.

It was further assumed in Kentucky that the bulk of the fighting, both on land and at sea, would be done by volunteer rather than regular forces. Primary reliance upon privately owned and armed vessels in the war at sea was expected to render the maintenance of an expanded American naval establishment superfluous. Kentuckians were supremely confident that on land the United States' numerically superior militia forces, spearheaded by small contingents of regulars, would easily overwhelm Britain's forces in Canada. Thus extensive preparations for war and heavy federal expenditures to support a greatly enlarged army and navy appeared unnecessary. The war, Kentuckians felt certain, would quickly be won by individual initiative and enterprise on the part of citizen-soldiers temporarily enrolled for a single, specific campaign.

To arguments that regular troops would be more responsive to national needs than militia and volunteers and could also be more easily directed toward the accomplishment of national objectives, Kentuckians paid scant heed. Regulars, they scoffed, were little better than hired mercenaries, prepared to fight wherever directed regardless of the cause. Men who fought only for pay, they contended, could never be relied upon to fight as effectively as militiamen who volunteered for service because their homes and their closest interests were directly involved in the outcome of the battle.

Kentuckians were not greatly concerned either by the knowledge that all but a small portion of the United States' enrolled militia were under state rather than federal authority. Lacking experience with any other mode of warfare, they assumed from the outset that for the United States the War of 1812 would more nearly resemble a number of disparate, sectional wars than a carefully concerted national campaign.

Kentucky's role in the American war effort was expected to be confined to an attack upon Upper Canada and to campaigns against Britain's Indian allies in the Northwest. When the war began all eyes in Kentucky were upon Fort Malden, the British post opposite Detroit. That small, frontier outpost commanded the route by which western land forces could most easily march into Upper Canada, and it was from there that Tecumseh's confederated tribes were supplied.

While it was possible in 1812 to raise larger numbers of men in the state than were immediately needed for the anticipated drive into Upper Canada, the assumption that Kentucky's military responsibility was limited to action in the Northwest caused Kentuckians to be extremely reluctant to volunteer for service elsewhere. Despite the importance of the Mississippi River to western commerce, they were even reluctant to serve at New Orleans, defense of which was considered to lie within Tennessee's and Louisiana's sphere of regional military responsibility. Soon after war was declared Richard M. Johnson assured President Madison that Kentucky volunteers, if called into action, would "go South, West or North." He made it plain, however, that Kentuckians preferred duty in the Northwest over assignment to the humid, fever-ridden lowlands of Louisiana partly "on account of health," but principally because of their eagerness to see Malden captured.

Kentuckians' preferences for campaigning north of the Ohio River were quickly confirmed by the success of various recruiting endeavors undertaken in the state. Upon his return to Lexington following the adjournment of Congress, Henry Clay reported to Secretary of State James Monroe that there was an abundance of volunteers for the contingent of 5,500 state militia being raised under federal authority for service in the Northwest. As of July 29, however, enlistments were far less numerous in military units that might be called upon to serve in other theaters of war.

To some small extent Kentuckians' decided preference for service in the Northwest can be explained by vengeful animosities arising out of a conviction that British agents from Canada had been responsible for instigating past Indian wars in the Ohio River Valley. Periodically after 1800, Kentucky orators and journalists reminded their audiences of Britain's alleged role in the bloody Indian wars of the 1790s and of their friends and relatives "who fell in those contests by the tomahawk or scalping knife of the merciless savage." But by 1812 the rapid spread of frontier settlement north of the Ohio River had long since rendered Kentucky immune from major Indian attacks. Indeed, prior to their experiences in the northwestern campaigns of 1812 and 1813, many Kentucky volunteers had never even seen an Indian.

Rather than revenge against England for past Indian atrocities, it was the prospect of striking a swift, decisive blow against British control in Upper Canada that most appealed to Kentuckians in 1812. Military expeditions raised in the state in the past had almost invariably been organized for the purpose of accomplishing a single, clearly specified objective within a limited period of time. The situation on the Detroit frontier at the beginning of the War of 1812 seemed ideally suited for successfully carrying out that type of military campaign with which Kentuckians were most familiar. That part of Upper Canada lying north of Lake Erie was known to be the most weakly defended portion of the sprawling British province. Although a considerable number of Indians were collected about Fort Malden, they were supported at the beginning of the war by only 150 British regulars and 300 Canadian militia. By eliminating Malden and its defenders, the war in Upper Canada could virtually be ended in a single blow. It was this expectation on the part of Kentucky volunteers to which a writer in the Paris *Western Citizen* referred when he wrote:

> *Oh how they long to rush into the field.*
> *Malden to seize, and make proud Britons yield;*
> *The governmental wheels to them move slow,*
> *They burn to crush the Lion at a blow.*

Unfortunately, the belief that victory over Britain would be swift was at once the most dominant aspect and the gravest flaw in the attitude with which the Kentucky public approached the War of 1812. It imparted a decidedly fragile quality to the enthusiasm Kentuckians displayed for the war. The confidence with which they celebrated the advent of hostilities made no concession to the possibility of unexpected adversities. The result was that Kentuckians, though burning with patriotic zeal at the commencement of the war, were psychologically unprepared for the long, bloody conflict that followed.

That the state was equally unready physically can also be attributed in large part to the assumption that Kentucky's role in the war would consist of supplying volunteers for a victorious dash into Upper Canada. According to returns made public by the War Department, Kentucky's enrolled militia force of 40,472 men was by far the largest in the trans-Appalachian West. But despite its size, there were serious shortcomings in the state's militia system. Infrequent militia musters provided no more than a minimal acquaintance with military maneuvers and inculcated even less discipline in the militia troops. The usual enlistment period of six months permitted little time to overcome these deficiencies in the field. Nor did it help that company officers, who were usually chosen by popular election, were often as inexperienced and ill-disciplined as the men they commanded. When Micah Taul, a future Kentucky congressman, was elected captain of his Wayne County militia company, he was almost totally unacquainted with military training. Taul was not even certain whether his name had ever before appeared on a militia muster role. His election as captain, however, depended little upon his knowledge of military maneuvers. Taul, in the opinion of his company, satisfactorily demonstrated his greater capacity for command in a vicious, no-holds-barred encounter with his opponent William Jones. "After a hard fight," Taul later recalled, "fist and skull, biting, gouging, etc, I came off victorious."

In other respects the Kentucky Militia was still less ready for war. Equipment, medicines, and even arms were in such short supply that as early as September 1812 Governor Isaac Shelby was turning away eager volunteers who could not arm and equip themselves. The means of supplying troops in the field with food and such supplies as were available were hopelessly inadequate, since no organized supply system existed. Quartermasters relied upon private contractors to purchase and transport supplies, with far from satisfactory results.

Although the probability of war was apparent by late 1811, the General Assembly did nothing of significance to correct these problems. Confident that Kentucky would be "insulated by distance" from the principal theaters of action in the approaching war, Shelby's predecessor, Governor Charles Scott, had asked only that the legislature attempt to purchase 5,000 stand of arms from Virginia in preparation for the conflict. No arms were procured, however. Accustomed since the Revolution to nothing more demanding than brief forays against local Indian tribes, few Kentucky legislators foresaw the need for a well-disciplined army or for a carefully prepared campaign in the Northwest.

Kentuckians also had little appreciation of the financial strain war would place upon the state. "In all the war talk [in the General Assembly] between 1809 and 1814," Kentucky historian Thomas D. Clark has written, "there was remarkably little sense of what it would cost to finance Kentucky's activities in the Northwest." The result was that the state's militia organization remained little more than a manpower pool from which to draw poorly trained and ill-equipped volunteers for short periods of active service.

Many Kentuckians appeared to believe in 1812 that the only step essential to readying the state for war was the election of a governor capable of organizing and administering Kentucky's war effort. That voters in the state were far more concerned with the outcome of the August gubernatorial election than with the November presidential election was a further indication of the highly decentralized manner in which they expected the war to be waged. Madison, as the Republican candidate, was the popular choice in Kentucky for reelection to the presidency. But in their search for a satisfactory gubernatorial candidate, many Kentuckians turned to former Governor Isaac Shelby, a veteran Indian fighter and a famed victor over the British in the Revolutionary War Battle of King's Mountain. Shelby, who had been Kentucky's first governor, was repeatedly urged to forsake retirement and assume the leadership of the state during the coming conflict.

When he reluctantly agreed to become a candidate the campaign in Shelby's behalf emphasized the Kentucky governor's responsibilities as commander-in-chief of the militia almost to the exclusion of his role as a civil administrator. "We are on the eve of a dangerous war, and the 'times that tried men's souls' are about to return," a pro-Shelby newspaper editorial reminded Kentucky voters early in the campaign. "The times therefore require a governor . . . with the head to plan and the hand to execute such measures as are essential to the public safety." Shelby's reputation as the hero of King's Mountain was used extensively and probably decisively in his favor during the campaign. His supporters derisively demanded to know where Shelby's opponent, Gabriel Slaughter, had fought "in the times of old Washington, when the sound was, *Liberty or Death!*" One partisan

Shelby backer in Bourbon County charged in the *Western Citizen* that *"Gabriel Slaughter* was then an INVA-LID! . . . and nothing more was the matter with him then, than is now." Would Kentucky voters consent, the writer wondered, "to put this same *invalid* at the head of all the militia in the state!"

Early predictions of "one universal burst of approbation" for Shelby's candidacy proved reasonably accurate. His victory in August was overwhelming. Three months later Madison also received a solid electoral vote from Kentucky, as had been confidently expected. In a number of counties Federalist presidential electors did not receive a single vote. In most other counties their tally was extremely small, as it was in Fayette County where Federalist electors polled only 11 percent of the vote.

Despite the enthusiasm for war that swept him into office in 1812, Isaac Shelby, together with Governor Charles Scott, Henry Clay, and others among the state's more experienced political leaders, was well aware that frustrated expectations of military success might cause abrupt changes in the public's mood. These men were also more familiar than many of their constituents with the peculiar characteristics of militia and volunteer troops. Past experiences had demonstrated to their satisfaction that under the right circumstances militiamen and volunteers often fought ferociously and effectively. But if conditions were not right they knew that militia and volunteer troops could frequently be unreliable. They believed clearly apparent goals, trusted leadership, and purposeful activity to be some of the conditions vital to successful performances by militia and volunteer units. For the sake of the public's and the army's morale, therefore, Shelby and some others among Kentucky's political leaders were extremely anxious to insure the existence of those particular conditions in the northwestern campaign.

It was for this reason that some state leaders, shortly after war was declared, began imploring administrative officials in Washington to make immediate use of Kentucky volunteers. Enforced idleness, they repeatedly warned, would cause war spirit to wane rapidly in the state. As early as July 24 Richard M. Johnson wrote President Madison, "The people of this State are accustomed to prompt & active measures. . . . If they should be disappointed in these expectations—I am sure great injury will be done to that noble & patriotic ardour which has prompted our people to volunteer."

For the same reason, Henry Clay urged Secretary of State James Monroe to use his influence to secure marching orders for the state's militia. Failure to order at least a portion of the Kentucky militia into the field, Clay advised, "is likely to create a degree of disappointment & mortification which it is impossible for me to describe, and I dread will eventuate in an utter disgust for volunteering. Indeed the consequences may be more injurious." Clay also appealed directly to Secretary of War William Eustis. "For God's sake," he begged on behalf of Kentucky's idle and increasingly discontented militiamen, "give them something to do." The fear among Kentucky volunteers that they would not be permitted "to share the glory, the toil & the danger" of the campaign to conquer Upper Canada was partially mollified when 2,000 of the state's federally authorized quota of 5,500 militia were finally ordered to reinforce General William Hull's army at Detroit.

Aware that confidence in their commanding officer could go far to ameliorate the effects of poor training and a lack of discipline in militia troops, influential public leaders in Kentucky were equally importunate in their pleas for the appointment of a popular and trusted figure to command the state's troops in the field. Neither the public nor the militia in Kentucky had confidence in Brigadier General James Winchester of Tennessee, who had been named by the War Department to command the Kentucky and Ohio reinforcements destined for Detroit. "Being a stranger and having the appearance of a supercilious officer, he was generally disliked," Private Elias Darnall recorded in his journal of the 1812–1813 campaign.

If anything, Private Darnall had understated the antipathy Kentucky militiamen felt toward service under Winchester. Their distaste for the unfortunate Tennessean was so strong that it occasionally manifested itself in unnerving pranks. "At one encampment," Private William B. Northcutt wrote in his diary, "they killed a porcupine and skined it and stretched the Skin over a pole that he used for a particular purpose in the night, and he went and sat down on it, and it like to have ruined him." At another encampment still greater damage was done to Winchester's dignity. "They sawed his pole that he had for the same purpose nearly in two," Private Northcutt affirmed, "so that when he went to use it in the night it broke intoo and let his generalship, Uniform and all fall Backwards in no very decent place, for I seen his Rigementals hanging high upon a place the next day taking the fresh air."

It was little wonder that the men responsible for organizing the state's war effort wanted Winchester superseded by a commander whom Kentucky troops were less reluctant to follow. The popular choice for a successor to Winchester was Governor William Henry Harrison, the hero of Tippecanoe and the most highly respected military figure in the Northwest. Harrison's popularity in Kentucky was attested by the enthusiasm with which he was greeted when he traveled from Louisville to Lexington in late June 1812. At the towns through which he passed crowds gathered to cheer the Indiana governor. Numerous public dinners were held in the state in his honor. His arrival at Frankfort on the twenty-sixth was announced by a "federal salute" from the local militia company. Prominent citizens in the state capital feted the victor of Tippecanoe at a local tavern where, according to reports in the *Palladium*, they "vied in their attentions to a man so highly esteemed throughout the state."

Harrison's visit provided an excellent opportunity for state leaders to urge the Indiana governor's qualifications for appointment to a military command upon the Madison administration. In a letter to Secretary of State Monroe, Henry Clay pointedly observed that Harrison's reception in Kentucky had been marked by "a cordiality and an attention which no public character ever before experienced in this Country." Citing Kentuckians' confidence in Harrison's ability to achieve swift victory in the Northwest as a reason, Clay and Governor Charles Scott exerted themselves in late July and early August to foster his appointment to command of the American forces in that theater. To President Madison, Scott wrote of Harrison: "It would give me the highest pleasure to see a man promoted to an efficient command, who promises to be one of the greatest military men of the time."

The War Department had given no indication of an intent to comply with these demands when, in mid-August, news arrived in Kentucky that General Hull's army was entrapped at Detroit. Consternation must have been the first reaction. William Hull had an army of between 2,000 and 2,200 regulars, Ohio militia, and Michigan volunteers at Detroit. At Malden reinforcements had brought British strength to 325 regulars, 850 Canadian militia, and about 400 Indians. Although inferior in land troops, the British had a small fleet that controlled Lake Erie, thus protecting Malden's left flank and threatening the American right. Nevertheless, Hull had on June 12 confidently moved the bulk of his army across the Detroit River onto Canadian soil. Issuing a proclamation implying that the Americans came as liberators and promising protection to Canadian sympathizers, Hull fortified his encampment and began bringing up supplies for an advance on Fort Malden.

Before Hull's preparations were completed, however, lightly garrisoned Fort Michilimackinac controlling the water passage between Lake Huron and Lake Michigan fell to a combined force of British, Canadians, and Indi-

ans. Discouraged by the possibility that Michilimackinac's fall would bring a flood of western Indians to support the British at Malden, Hull also found his own long
line of supplies and communications increasingly threatened. Using the mobility that control of Lake Erie gave
them to the best advantage, British detachments were
crossing to the American side almost at will and joining
with Tecumseh's warriors to cut the long wilderness
tracks connecting Detroit with its supply bases in Ohio.
After several attempts to reopen his supply routes failed,
Hull ignominiously retreated from Canada to his Detroit
fortress. There his army remained, unable to move and
faced with the prospect of slow strangulation.

Along with official news of the plight of Hull's army,
Governor Charles Scott received a request to hasten
forward the Kentucky contingent of reinforcements destined for Detroit. But the same dirt-bespattered messen-
ger who came galloping into Frankfort bearing these
dispatches also brought a number of private letters to
Scott from subordinate officers at Detroit. Each of these
letters predicted complete disaster on the northwestern
frontier, unless the elderly, overcautious Hull was sup-
planted by a commander of greater ability. They had the
effect of making Scott and others more determined than
ever that Kentuckians in the Northwest Army should fight
under a competent commanding officer in whom they
had confidence and trust.

Although Scott's term in office was to end a few days
later on August 25, he unhesitatingly initiated immediate
actions intended to circumvent General James Winchester's authority over Kentucky troops in the Northwest.
Most of Kentucky's political leaders could be expected to
be in Frankfort to honor Scott upon his retirement from
office and to see the new governor inaugurated. Availing
himself of this opportunity, Scott issued invitations to
Governor-elect Shelby, former Governor Christopher
Greenup, Supreme Court Justice Thomas Todd, General
Samuel Hopkins, Henry Clay, and Richard M. Johnson to

meet with him on his last day in office and agree upon the best plan to adopt in the emergency. When the meeting took place, the conferees first decided that the strength of the detachment of Kentucky reinforcements destined for Detroit should be increased from the 2,000 men authorized by the War Department to 3,400 men. More importantly, they unanimously agreed that William Henry Harrison should be authorized to command the detachment. Technically, it was unconstitutional to appoint a resident of another state an officer in the Kentucky militia. But Kentucky's political leaders were so convinced that popular leadership was crucial to successful performances by militia and volunteers, that they were prepared to set constitutional scruples aside. The legal obstacle was quickly skirted by bestowing upon Harrison a brevet rather than a regular commission as major general in the Kentucky militia.

The participants in the conference were well aware that their action created an intolerable division in command over the relief expedition forming in Kentucky and at Cincinnati. With Harrison's appointment to the command of all Kentucky troops, Winchester was left with undisputed jurisdiction over only a single regiment of regulars. It was intended by the conferees that this situation should ultimately force the Madison administration to choose between Harrison and Winchester. "This arrangement," Shelby pointed out to Secretary of State Monroe a few days after the conference of August 25, "at once divides the army under governor Harrison, and renders either part unequal to any object of importance and ruins the fairest prospects of the expedition." Shelby's implication that the federal government should respond to the action taken in Kentucky by vesting sole command in Harrison seems clear. But if Madison still had doubts about what was desired by the Kentucky leadership, a letter to the president from Judge Todd must have removed them. Todd bluntly informed Madison on September 2: "Harrison is now with the army making active preparations to retrieve our losses—the officers and soldiers in high spirits having the fullest confidence in the Genl . . . . Winchester's presence will damp this ardour."

By the time Todd penned his letter to Madison, the military situation in the Northwest had become extremely serious for the United States. Although communications were very slow in 1812, Kentuckians had learned by early September that on August 16 Hull had surrendered his army and Detroit to the British. Shortly afterward, still another American post near the Canadian frontier had surrendered. The small garrison at Fort Dearborn had laid down their arms and marched out as prisoners of war, only to be slaughtered among the sand dunes along the southern shores of Lake Michigan by the Indian allies of their British captors. With the fall of Michilimackinac, Detroit, and Fort Dearborn, the American line of defense against the British and Indians west of Ohio was thrown back almost to Vincennes, the capital of Indiana Territory. The army ordered to relieve Detroit suddenly became the only American army in the Northwest.

It was with redoubled "ardour," therefore, that the Kentucky public learned on September 8 of Harrison's appointment to the command of state troops in the field. The *Kentucky Gazette* announced the news under the headline "Huzza for the Hero of Tippecanoe." The article that followed declared: "Now, the backwoodsmen are satisfied. Now, they can, with confidence, rally round the standard of their country." When the newly brevetted major general joined his troops at Cincinnati he was greeted with demonstrations of the "utmost joy." The obvious preference of Kentucky militiamen for service under Harrison, their equally obvious reluctance to be led by Winchester, and Harrison's own refusal to accept any United States' commission that would leave him subordinate to the Tennessean increased the pressure upon the Madison administration to choose between the two rivals for command of the Northwest Army.

Meanwhile Governor Shelby, in office less than two weeks, was going still further in his efforts to insure local direction of the war in the Northwest. Not content merely to promote the appointment of a popular western figure to command in the field, Shelby was concerned about the effects lack of confidence in officials at higher levels might have upon the western war effort. Secretary of War William Eustis, whom Madison had appointed for political reasons rather than ability, inspired as little confidence among Kentuckians as did Winchester. Shortly after the fall of Detroit, therefore, Shelby recommended a plan to Eustis that would have permitted westerners to direct the campaign against Upper Canada independent of control by the War Department.

The principal feature of Shelby's audacious proposal was that authority over military operations in the Northwest should be vested in "a board of respectable characters, resident in the western country." The board would be authorized to plan and conduct all offensive and defensive campaigns in the Northwest. All federal quartermasters and other agents in that theater would be placed under its control, and the board would be empowered to draw upon federal stores for supplies and munitions without reference to the War Department. This proposal would have effectively stripped Eustis of his ability either to control or to interfere with military operations in the Northwest. For as Shelby described it, the board's only obligation to the secretary of war would be "to report to the department of war, from time to time, the measures by them adopted."

In arguing for the adoption of his plan, Shelby pointed out that the Indiana and Illinois territories might well be overrun by hostile Indians, unless defended by Kentucky troops. But his principal concern was admittedly for public morale in the state, if the direction of war operations remained in distant hands. He feared that the logistical difficulties of directing military operations in the West from Washington would "perplex both officers and soldiers, have a tendency to disgust men with the service, and in a long tedious war render it difficult for the government to call forth those resources, which the exigency of the case may require." He cited the failure of supplies, and especially pay, to arrive on schedule at designated places as potential irritants to Kentucky volunteers. If the secretary of war insisted upon retaining control over military operations in the Northwest, Shelby declared, he was "induced to believe" that the Northwest Army's attempts to regain lost ground would come to naught. "And, what I most apprehend and dread," he repeated, "a dissatisfaction among our citizens to the great cause, [might arise] from some of the reasons heretofore assigned."

Shelby was disappointed in his hope that Eustis would relinquish federal authority over military operations in the Northwest to the extent that the Kentucky governor had proposed. But on September 24 at Piqua on the route north, Harrison received a dispatch informing him that Madison had acceded to public opinion in Kentucky and the Northwest and had granted him command of the Northwest Army. Harrison was further informed that the army under his command was to be expanded to a force of eight to ten thousand men. And from Secretary of War Eustis, Shelby received assurances that Harrison would be authorized to exercise many of the powers Shelby would have vested in his western war board. The War Department, Eustis promised, would cooperate in every possible way with Harrison's efforts to recapture Detroit and conquer Upper Canada.

Insofar as they understood the existing problems, Kentucky political leaders had done everything possible to organize the state for war during the first months of hostilities. Many undetected deficiencies in the state's militia system would be tragically revealed in the months of combat that lay ahead. But astute statesmen such as

Scott, Shelby, Johnson, Clay, and a few others had clearly recognized that the enthusiasm with which Kentuckians welcomed news of war did not necessarily indicate that the public was psychologically prepared for a contest that might well prove to be longer and more difficult than generally expected.

These same statesmen had, therefore, acted effectively to establish in the Northwest those conditions deemed most favorable to achieving public expectations of a swift, victorious dash into Upper Canada. Despite the early, wholly unexpected defeats inflicted upon the United States in the Northwest during the fall of 1812, the goal of conquering Upper Canada remained the constant and readily apparent objective both of Kentucky's people and of the state's leaders. Beyond this, Kentucky political leaders used every measure of their influence with the Madison administration to accomplish three ends. First, they insisted that Kentucky volunteers should be brought into action at the earliest opportunity so that war spirit would not be dissipated in the state from a lack of purposeful activity. They then brought extensive pressure upon the Madison administration to appoint as commander of the Northwest Army the one man under whom Kentucky militia and volunteers seemed likely to fight with the greatest zest and effectiveness. And finally, they urged the administration to grant that commander or other western leaders the broadest conceivable latitude in organizing and directing military operations in the Northwest.

To accomplish these purposes, Henry Clay and other Kentucky leaders had repeatedly appealed to Secretary of State Monroe to intercede with both the president and the War Department. Shortly after the decision had been made in Washington to place Harrison above Winchester in command of the Northwest Army and to give him broad authority in organizing the western war effort, Monroe assured Clay that the efforts of Kentucky's political leaders had been influential in the arrangements made for conducting northwestern military operations. "You & our other friends in Kentucky," Secretary Monroe wrote, "will find the utmost attention has been paid to your opinions & wishes, on all these subjects."

3

REMEMBER THE RAISIN!

Despite Governor Shelby's concern for public morale, war spirit in Kentucky was unaffected by the early defeats inflicted upon the United States in the Northwest. Kentuckians were shocked by the surrender of Detroit and the capture of Forts Michilimackinac and Dearborn. But they remained highly confident that the losses would soon be retrieved and Canada conquered. The setbacks suffered on the Canadian border were attributed almost entirely to Hull's personal unsuitability for command. "Of Hull's treachery scarcely a doubt is entertained in this Country," Henry Clay wrote to Secretary Monroe in September 1812. For his own part, Clay considered Hull's capitulation "so shameful, so disgraceful a surrender," that it made little difference whether it resulted from treachery or cowardice. Hull, in his opinion, deserved to be shot.

Regardless of whether these charges were entirely justified, the military situation in the Northwest was extremely grave in the dark days of early September. The entire Illinois and Indiana frontier lay exposed to attack by the victorious British and Indian forces at Detroit. That the situation did not worsen was due in part to the cool heroism of twenty-seven-year-old Zachary Taylor, a Kentuckian and a captain in the United States Army.

Along the line of the Wabash River in Indiana Territory, all that stood between the eager Indians and the territorial capital of Vincennes was crudely constructed, fever-ridden Fort Harrison. Since shortly before the declaration of war, Zachary Taylor, with a small detachment from the Seventh Infantry Regiment, had been in command of the stockaded post. As the British and Indian cordon around Detroit tightened the whole frontier grew tense. The blow that Taylor expected to be struck against Fort Harrison with the "full of the moon" in early August failed to materialize. By September, however, a dozen male civilians and nine women and children had sought safety within the small, primitive, log fort.

Fort Harrison seemed capable of providing little more than a semblance of the protection the alarmed settlers desired. Taylor himself was not yet fully recovered from a fever that had left all but six privates and two noncommissioned officers from among his small garrison bedridden. Including the civilians, Taylor could muster no more than fifteen physically fit men to defend Fort Harrison, when four distant musket shots warned of approaching danger on the evening of September 3, 1812. Too few to risk venturing forth to discover the cause of the shots, the waiting men paced along the walls through the long night, their weapons constantly at the ready. With the morning, the scalped, mutilated bodies of two men who had been cutting hay a quarter-mile from the post were discovered. The siege that Taylor had long expected had begun.

Late in the afternoon, a delegation of Indian emissaries emerged from the woods and approached the fort under a flag of truce. Protesting their peaceful intentions, they stated that one of their number would return the following day to negotiate for food for their starving brothers at Prophet's Town. That night Taylor doled out extra rounds of ammunition to the defenders of Fort Harrison and cautioned the guards to be alert for treachery. All was quiet until shortly before midnight. Suddenly an alarm gun fired by one of the sentries shattered the stillness and brought Taylor racing from his quarters. In the darkness Indian warriors had stealthily crept to the very walls of the beleaguered fort. Reaching through small cracks between the logs, they had set fire to the store of food and whiskey housed in the blockhouse that formed the southwest corner of the fort. Already flames were leaping toward the blockhouse's tinder-dry roof.

As the few able-bodied men began desperately ripping away the burning roof to avert a general conflagration, Taylor ordered the convalescents and women formed into a bucket brigade. At that moment the encircling Indians opened upon the fort with all the weapons at their disposal. Hastily, every soldier who could be spared was diverted by Taylor to the defense of the fort, while others continued to fight the spreading flames roaring around the southwest blockhouse.

Firing from behind the sheltering walls, Taylor's riflemen beat back the first wild charge by several hundred painted warriors. But the fight continued to rage almost unabated as bands of leaping, howling red men dashed again and again at the stoutly defended fortress. First one man and then a second was shot from the exposed roof of the blazing blockhouse. Children cried and women screamed, even as they lugged the heavy water buckets toward the burning structure. In the din and confusion two men panicked, leaped the wall, and fled into the darkness. A bullet found Private William Cowan, and he fell dead at his post. A settler was killed. Several others were wounded. Taylor held the survivors steadfast, however, and directed their activities with good effect.

The southwest blockhouse was beyond saving, but gradually the fire's spread was checked. Through great effort enough logs were pulled together to fill the smoldering gap in the palisade with a low breastwork. Despite their repeated charges, the swarming Indians were held at bay. As dawn approached the hail of shots and arrows from beyond the walls slowed, and the assailants of Fort Harrison soon faded into the woods.

But the Indians had not gone. For days Taylor and his weary men watched for signs of a renewed attack. With most of their provisions consumed in the blockhouse fire, the hungry survivors subsisted on green corn. Driven by the need for provisions, Taylor reluctantly sent two soldiers out on September 10, hoping that they could escape down the Wabash by boat and carry word of the fort's plight to Vincennes. They were back within hours to report that the Indians had built fires along the banks and were lying in wait for any messengers attempting to run the river gauntlet. Two nights later a second pair of messengers sent by Taylor succeeded in slipping through the woods, evading the Indian sentinels, and eventually reaching the territorial capital.

Unknown to Taylor, a relieving force was already on its way. His messengers arrived at Vincennes to learn that over a thousand Indiana and Kentucky troops under Colonel William Russell were moving by forced marches to the aid of the besieged outpost. Although his provision train was attacked en route and most of its small escort killed, Colonel Russell's main body of rangers and militiamen reached Fort Harrison on September 16.

After more than a week the siege was broken and much of the Indiana and Illinois frontier was saved from the fury of savage warfare. The successful defense of Fort Harrison was the first land victory for the United States in the War of 1812. It stemmed the collapse of American defenses in the Northwest, dispelled some of the gloom cast by the surrender of Hull's army, and won for Zachary Taylor (who was raised to the brevet rank of major) the first brevet commission ever awarded by the government of the United States.

Meanwhile Governor Shelby, from his office in Frankfort, was taking energetic steps in the wake of the Detroit debacle to hold the Indians in check on the frontier and to help retrieve the situation on the Canadian border. Dispatch riders were sent galloping northward with letters urging Harrison to drive straight for Detroit with the forces already under his command. At the same time, without waiting for authorization from the War Department, Shelby called for 2,000 mounted Kentucky volunteers to march under Major General Samuel Hopkins against Tecumseh's hostile followers in Indiana and Illinois. Hopkins's instructions from Shelby were to raid deep into the Indians' own country, destroying food supplies and, if possible, drawing warriors away from Harrison's path of advance and to the defense of their threatened villages.

The response to Shelby's call for volunteers clearly evidenced that Kentuckians had lost none of their initial enthusiasm for the war as a result of Hull's surrender. The men under Hopkins were to be a volunteer force in the strictest sense of the term. Lacking authorization for the expedition from the War Department, Shelby could not enter them for federal service. Nor did the thirty-day period of enlistment count toward fulfilling the volunteers' obligation for active service in the state militia. Men who offered their services for the expedition were even required to outfit themselves, since Shelby had no arms, equipment, or blankets to give them.

Nevertheless, volunteers responded readily to the crisis created by the capitulation of Detroit. "Parties are daily passing to the theatre of action," Henry Clay testified. "Last night 70 lay on my farm, and they go on from a solitary individual to companies of 10—50—100 &c." Many of the volunteers were among the most "influential and eloquent & respectable characters" in Kentucky. Of the high quality of the troops led by Hopkins, Shelby wrote: "I have never seen such a body of men in the western country or anywhere else."

But the fervor with which Kentuckians supported the fall campaign of 1812 was not destined to last. Like their response to the declaration of war against England, it was predicated upon excessive expectations of subduing the Indians and recapturing Detroit in a single campaign. When those expectations were disappointed, the enthusiasm which Kentuckians had maintained for military service since the inception of the war began to give way to disillusionment.

The deterioration of war spirit in the state began with the failure of the Hopkins expedition. That expedition, from which so much had been expected, foundered on the rocks of ineffective organization, ill discipline, and lack of training. With only thirty days in which to accomplish the goals of the expedition, there was no time to weld the force into a cohesive unit. The best that Hopkins could do before leaving Kentucky was to arrange hastily the inexperienced volunteers into five loosely organized regiments. His plan was to reprovision his troops at Fort Harrison, a hundred miles above Vincennes, and from there move against the hostile Indian villages in Illinois Territory. But by the time the mounted volunteers arrived at Fort Harrison on October 14, the high spirits evident in Kentucky had evaporated. Unconditioned for long, hard days on horseback, a number of individuals had already abandoned the expedition. Many of the remainder were saddle-weary and sullen.

Nevertheless, with ten days' rations and two guides the little army broke camp the following morning and headed deep into Indian country. In four days they covered better than 120 miles without discovering the Kickapoo and Peoria villages that they intended to destroy. With their rations rapidly dwindling, it was increasingly clear to the volunteers that even the guides were lost. A fifth day of fruitless searching was capped by a prairie fire that threatened to consume the camp. Although the camp was saved by dint of great exertions through the night, the last vestiges of morale were completely broken.

By morning, Hopkins was faced with a choice between retreat or an open mutiny. The disappointed general's pleas for as few as 500 men to continue with him were rebuffed. Many of his officers stood firmly behind Hopkins, but almost unanimously their men voted to return to Fort Harrison. With his authority destroyed, there was nothing left for Hopkins except to place himself at the rear of the column, presumably the point of greatest danger, and trail his broken-spirited men back to the Wabash. Although Hopkins's conduct was completely exonerated by Shelby, and later by a board of inquiry, the failure of the expedition was discouraging to the volunteers and disappointing to the Kentucky public.

Elsewhere on the frontier, the inability of Harrison's Northwest Army to advance rapidly against Detroit soon became a still greater source of disillusionment to Kentucky hopes for swift, decisive victories over the British and their Indian allies. Harrison's plan for the campaign divided the army into three columns and directed each to march by a separate route to the Rapids of the Maumee River, which flowed north into Lake Erie. There the three columns were to be reunited for an assault on Detroit.

Whereas the Kentucky public, in their anticipation of early successes, could ignore the difficulties of terrain in the Northwest and the lateness of the season, Harrison's army could not. Almost from the outset heavy autumn rains turned roads and forest tracks in northern Indiana and Ohio into quagmires. Under these conditions troop movements quickly became difficult and adequate provisioning of the advancing army nearly impossible. As autumn rains turned to snow and freezing weather, the progress of the right and center columns was slowed to a barely perceptible crawl. On the left General James Winchester's command was brought to a complete halt on the upper Maumee River, miles short of their destination. There they remained from October until early January.

Having received no advance pay with which to purchase uniforms, most of the Kentucky volunteers in Harrison's army had begun the campaign "thinly clad . . . and believing too that they would be in Canada before the winter set in." This aspiration dwindled as the campaign lengthened. With the hope of action fading and suffering from hunger and exposure, the militiamen became weary of slow movements that seemed to get nowhere.

Discontent became particularly rife at Winchester's encampment on the upper Maumee. There in mid-December subordinate officers in the unpopular Tennessean's command were forced to use every possible argument to suppress open mutiny. "We have here been exposed to numberless difficulties, as well as deprived of the common necessaries of life," Private Elias Darnall wrote in explanation of the militiamen's rebellious mood. "And what made these things operate more severely was, all hopes of obtaining any conquest was entirely abandoned." Like many other militiamen who had volunteered for the campaign, Private Darnall wondered if it would not be better to disband the army until spring rather than continue.

Through October and into November the Kentucky press continued to publish optimistic reports predicting the recapture of Detroit in the near future. By December, however, the public was becoming aware of the difficulties and drudgery of campaigning in the Northwest. Letters from soldiers at the front and more realistic press appraisals of the Northwest Army's plight caused widespread concern for the suffering Kentucky volunteers. Then came news of a fresh disaster at Frenchtown on the Raisin River.

During the first weeks of January 1813, Winchester had succeeded in building sleds and moving his force of nearly 1,300 Kentuckians down the frozen Maumee to the rendezvous point at the Rapids. There at old Fort Defiance he was informed that approximately fifty Canadian militia and one hundred Indians were guarding a considerable quantity of provisions at Frenchtown, thirty-five miles away on the Raisin River. Although the remainder of Harrison's Northwest Army had not yet arrived, Winchester called his officers together for a council of war. Despite the deep snow and the close proximity of Fort Malden, only eighteen miles beyond Frenchtown, it was decided that an immediate attempt should be made to capture the British stores.

The next day, January 16, 550 Kentucky militiamen under Lieutenant Colonel William Lewis and 100 under Lieutenant Colonel John Allen set out for Frenchtown. For a day and a half the shivering, thinly clad Kentuckians struggled through the snowbound woods and over the ice along the frozen shore of Lake Erie. They reached the south bank of the River Raisin between two and three o'clock on the afternoon of January 18. As they emerged from the woods the loud report of a single, three-pound howitzer located across the river warned them that the enemy was alert to their approach.

Against the obstinate resistance of a slightly larger force than anticipated, the Kentuckians formed a line of battle, crossed the river, and pressed their attack. Adept at skirmishing in wooded terrain, the Canadians and Indians gave ground slowly and the fight continued for several hours. By dusk the Kentuckians had succeeded in pushing the smaller enemy force only about two miles into the woods beyond Frenchtown and had inflicted only limited losses upon them. About a dozen Indian bodies were scattered through the trampled battle area, and two prisoners had been taken. When the failing light forced Lewis and Allen to break off the engagement, the Kentucky losses were twelve dead and fifty-five wounded.

Having occupied Frenchtown, Lewis reported to Winchester and requested reinforcements. The danger of a counterattack by British forces from Detroit or nearby Malden was immediately evident, and Winchester moved quickly to consolidate his army. Leaving 300 men under Brigadier General John Payne at Fort Defiance on the Maumee, he marched the remainder of his militia troops rapidly toward Frenchtown. Colonel Samuel Wells's Seventeenth United States Infantry detachment, 250 regulars all recruited in Kentucky, followed close behind. With their arrival on January 20, the total strength of Winchester's command at Frenchtown was close to 1,000.

Frenchtown proved to be a small settlement of thirty-three families. To the north it was protected by a single row of timber pickets that lapped around the town in a rough semicircle. The River Raisin flowed past on the south, although the pickets did not extend all the way to the river's edge. By the time Wells's regulars arrived, the space within the pickets was entirely occupied by militia units. Wells was accordingly ordered by Winchester to make his camp in an open field 100 yards to the right of the pickets. With only ten rounds of ammunition per man, the infantrymen had nothing to protect them in an attack except a rail fence. Winchester, meanwhile, took up residence in a house located a mile or more above the settlement and on the opposite side of the river.

At Malden, General Henry Proctor had received word of the first engagement at Frenchtown as soon as or sooner than had Winchester. While Winchester was moving reinforcements to the Raisin River and writing reports to Harrison, whose troops began arriving at Fort Defiance the same day Winchester reached Frenchtown, Proctor was gathering his forces at Malden. When the Kentuckians at Frenchtown went to sleep on the night of January 21, Proctor and 597 British regulars and Canadian militia were less than five miles away. With them were 600 to 800 Indians led by the Wyandot chief, Roundhead. Striking camp before dawn the next day, Proctor had his troops and three small fieldpieces in position to attack Frenchtown by first light. Surprise was complete in the American camp when the British struck.

Although Proctor had the advantage of slightly greater numbers, his greatest advantage lay in his three small artillery pieces. The marksmanship of the Kentucky militiamen sheltered behind the pickets wreaked havoc among British units that came within range of their deadly rifles. But Wells's regulars, lying beyond the picketed area, were completely exposed to the fire of the British howitzers. With no artillery of their own, they were soon cut to pieces. Worse still, there was nothing on which to

49

anchor the right side of their line. And when they attempted to withdraw to escape the maelstrom of canister and grape shot hurled by the British howitzers, they found themselves outflanked by Indians and Canadian militia.

Since they were unable to regroup under the deadly hail of cannon and musket fire, the withdrawal of the regulars toward the riverbank gradually became a rout. Colonel Allen and Colonel Lewis each led militia companies out to stiffen the resistance of the American right and provide a rallying point for the disorganized regulars. Their companies also wilted and then disintegrated under the British fire. Pounded by artillery and hotly pursued by Indians, both militia and regulars became panic-stricken. Singly and in small groups, they fled across the River Raisin and into the woods on the south bank. General Winchester, from his headquarters up the river, arrived on the scene just in time to be swept along in the general rout of the American right.

Few of the fleeing Kentuckians escaped. Many were killed and scalped by Indians who had circled around to cut off the retreat; others were overtaken by their pursuers. Nearly a hundred fell in one small area. Captain John Simpson, who had forsaken the safety of his seat in Congress for the field of battle, was among the slain. Colonel Allen, though wounded in the thigh, followed his fleeing troops nearly two miles in an effort to rally them and return them to the fight. When this proved impossible, he calmly seated himself upon a log to await the pursuing Indians, one of whom he struck down with his sword before being killed. Colonel Lewis and General Winchester were more fortunate. Captured by Indians, they were taken through the snow to Roundhead, who had them stripped and delivered as prisoners to Proctor.

The battle, however, was not yet ended. Major George Madison, now in command of the Kentucky militiamen within the picketed area around Frenchtown, had thus far not lost a man. The regulars who had formed the right flank of his position, and those militia companies who had gone to their assistance, had been crushed. The commanding general of the Kentucky forces at Frenchtown had been captured. There was no way to reply to the British artillery pieces playing upon the picketed area from beyond effective rifle range. But Madison had no thought of surrender.

Of more immediate concern to Madison than the British artillery fire was a tall double barn overlooking his position from a distance of about 150 yards. Enemy marksmen, by taking possession of the unoccupied barn, could fire directly into the Kentuckians sheltering behind the low pickets. Although there was no way to reach the barn without crossing open fields under the direct fire of a line of British regulars on one side and a band of Indian warriors on the other, Madison called for a volunteer to burn the structure. His call was answered by Ensign William O. Butler.

With a stick of blazing firewood in one hand, Butler vaulted the low pickets and raced across the open fields toward the barn. Musket balls whipped around him from two directions as British and Indians alike turned their fire upon him. None found him. Breathless but untouched, Butler reached the looming building and thrust his burning brand into a pile of hay. Scarcely pausing to consider the danger, he flung himself out the door and began his dash back across the open field. Part way to the safety of his own lines, Butler realized with dismay that the fire had not caught.

Ignoring the muskets banging at him from left and right, Butler turned and again made his way to the barn. From the British lines, fleet Indian warriors were already running toward the rear of the building to head him off and save the structure from the torch. Kneeling over the smoldering pile of hay, Butler fanned the dying sparks into a roaring blaze. The mounting flames frustrated the Indians' attempts to enter the barn from the rear, as Butler bounded out the front and ran once more across the field. His clothing ripped by passing bullets but otherwise unharmed, the daring ensign tumbled across the pickets to safety. Moments later, as he stood catching his breath, a musket ball hit him in the chest and knocked him unconscious to the ground. The ball that struck Butler was fortunately spent, however, and he survived the battle at the River Raisin to become a candidate for governor of Kentucky in 1844.

Meanwhile behind the British lines, Proctor was skillfully playing upon Winchester's fears of Indian vengeance if American resistance continued. Though a prisoner and no longer in command of the Frenchtown garrison, Winchester sent a note to Madison under flag of truce ordering him to surrender. Madison was assured that his men would be protected against the Indians, that they would be treated as prisoners of war with the right to retain private property, and that their side arms would eventually be restored.

Madison's command was now completely surrounded by a superior force. His store of ammunition was also nearly depleted. Soon there would be no choice but surrender or a hopeless fight to the last man with knives and clubbed rifles. But Madison mistrusted the assurances given Winchester by Proctor. Not until additional guarantees of protection for his men were obtained directly from Proctor would he agree to order his troops to lay down their weapons. After surrendering, the suspicious Madison continued to keep his men together in a body on the march north to Malden. His orders, even though his men were unarmed, were to resist by force any attempt by Indians to infiltrate their ranks and circulate among them.

In all probability Madison's determination saved the lives of some of his men. The battle was ended by midday, and Proctor insisted upon marching without delay for Malden. During the course of the march Indians hovered constantly around the dejected line of defeated

Kentuckians. Numerous prisoners were threatened or beaten, and some were killed with tomahawk or knife without intervention by the British guards. Many others were spirited away from the line of march and taken to distant villages far beyond Malden and Detroit.

But the worst was yet to come. Proctor had ordered about eighty of the Kentucky wounded left at Frenchtown until sleighs or other transport could be provided to carry them to Malden. Their fate was entrusted to a party of fifty or more Indians, who were to serve as guards. Only four or five British soldiers were assigned as guards and interpreters. After the army's departure, the Indians found whiskey among the stores of provisions in the settlement. During the course of a drunken victory celebration on the night of January 22–23, they murdered many of the severely wounded prisoners in their beds and set fire to the houses in which they were sheltered. Altogether, between forty and sixty-five of the prisoners were killed and scalped. With few exceptions, the survivors were carried away by Indians into captivity.

According to their reports, which did not include Indian casualties, the British lost 24 dead and 161 wounded in the Battle of the River Raisin. How many Kentucky casualties were sustained has never been accurately ascertained. Fewer than a hundred, possibly no more than thirty or forty from Winchester's command, escaped and made their way to Harrison's headquarters on the Maumee. Some of those carried into captivity by the Indians were ransomed by sympathetic Detroit residents; a few managed to escape and returned to Kentucky months or even years later; others never came back. Of the prisoners marched off by Proctor, fewer than 500 were eventually released. The best estimates thus indicate that at least 400 Kentuckians were killed in the battle or by the Indians immediately afterwards. These losses were not forgotten. The battle cry "Remember the Raisin!" rang loudly across every battlefield on which Kentuckians subsequently fought in the War of 1812.

Governor Shelby was attending a theatrical performance in Frankfort, when a message reached him about eight o'clock in the evening of February 2 describing the defeat and massacre at the River Raisin. The distress caused by the loss of an entire army of Kentuckians was deep. "This melancholy event has filled the state with mourning, and every feeling heart bleeds with anguish," Shelby wrote Harrison. Students at Transylvania College in Lexington resolved to wear black crepe for thirty days in memory of the River Raisin dead. And the General Assembly, which had been on the point of adjournment, prolonged its session an extra day to authorize the enlistment of another 3,000 militia in the event that they were needed at the front.

Despite many patriotic protestations of determination to avenge the defeat, the River Raisin massacre and its consequences were a blow to war spirit in the state. Early illusions of a swift, virtually unopposed dash into Upper Canada were entirely dispelled. Harrison's advance against Detroit was halted indefinitely by the destruction of the left wing of his Northwest Army. For the Kentucky volunteer the character of the war in the Northwest underwent a change. The campaign against Upper Canada settled into a grinding, unspectacular routine of road building, fortifying, and garrison duty. Kentuckians, who had anticipated few hardships and much glory in the conquest of Upper Canada, were unprepared for the change and were slow to adjust to it.

4

THE FATE OF WAR

Disillusionment with American prospects for conquering Canada continued to deepen in Kentucky during the early months of 1813. Although public attitudes in the state were more directly affected by events in the Northwest than elsewhere, the failure of the first northwestern campaign was not alone responsible. Nowhere could there be found a cause for encouragement in the existing military situation.

As late as August 1812 Thomas Jefferson had written: "The acquisition of Canada this year, as far as the neighborhood of Quebec, will be a mere matter of marching, and will give us experience for . . . the final expulsion of England from the American continent." At that time large numbers of Kentuckians wholeheartedly had shared Jefferson's confidence. But every subsequent American attempt to launch an invasion of Canada during the 1812–1813 campaign season ended in failure or defeat.

Twelve days after Jefferson penned his prediction of easy conquests, Hull had surrendered Detroit and nearly 1,100 men. On October 13 General Stephen Van Rensselaer lost an army nearly as large in an attack against Queenston on the Canadian side of the Niagara River. In mid-November, General Henry Dearborn led a large militia force north by way of Lake Champlain to the Canadian border, only to have his men refuse to follow farther on the grounds that militia could not be constitutionally required to fight outside the United States. Before the month was out a second effort to enter Canada along the Niagara River frontier ended in hasty withdrawal. Harrison's decision temporarily to abandon offensive operations against Upper Canada following the destruction of the Northwest Army's left wing at River Raisin thus climaxed an extremely frustrating campaign season for the United States.

Events in Washington, meanwhile, were causing many Kentuckians to believe that the spring of 1813 would bring little improvement in American prospects for victory. After convening for its second session on November 2, 1812, the Twelfth Congress of the United States had immediately proceeded to devote most of its time to formulating plans for enlarging the navy and for reorganizing and reinforcing the army. During December and early January Kentucky observers were satisfied that the nation's lawmakers were strenuously seeking means to prosecute the war more effectively. In late January, however, the House Foreign Relations Committee reported a bill to Congress that excited grave doubts in Kentucky about congressional steadfastness in the war.

Kentuckians were still reeling from the first news of the disaster at Frenchtown, when accounts of the Foreign Relations Committee's report were published by leading state newspapers. The committee's report asserted that Britain's repeal of the restrictions imposed upon neutral American shipping, news of which had arrived in the United States shortly after hostilities were declared, left impressment as the only major issue in the war. The committee reasoned, therefore, that peace might be restored between the two nations on the basis of a settlement of the impressment question alone. Other American grievances against England, the committee argued, could be settled in postwar negotiations. To pave the way for peace talks and a speedier end to hostilities, the committee recommended to Congress the so-called Seamen's bill. The purpose of the bill was to facilitate a resolution of the impressment controversy by promising a reduction in the number of British subjects employed on American vessels immediately following the conclusion of a peace treaty.

Kentuckians who had long argued that American grievances against England ran far deeper than impressment and the confiscation of American ships and cargoes were dismayed. Although a majority of Kentucky's combined House and Senate delegation supported the Seamen's bill, the reaction to the measure in the state was almost entirely adverse. Kentucky newspapers were filled with editorials and letters condemning the Foreign Relations Committee's report and denying that impressment was the only issue in the war. To agree to a treaty of peace that failed to protect American rights against every form of British encroachment, Kentucky critics contended, would be tantamount to a surrender of national sovereignty. When Congress adopted the Foreign Relations Committee's proposals on February 27, the news provoked heated charges that the nation's lawmakers were more inclined to petition for peace than to provide adequate means for winning the war. The suspicion that the federal government was reluctant to continue the war spread rapidly in Kentucky and contributed significantly to the growing disillusionment with American war efforts that gripped the state in early 1813.

Suspicions of congressional weakness in prosecuting the war soon bred suspicions of weakness in the Madison administration as well. In reassessing the reasons for Harrison's inability to recover lost ground after the surrender of Detroit, Kentuckians laid much blame upon the executive branch of government. As early as December 1812 Henry Clay had confided his doubts about Madison's abilities as a war president to Caesar A. Rodney of Delaware. "Mr. Madison is wholly unfit for war," Clay wrote. "Nature has cast him in too benevolent a mould. . . . He is not fit for the rough and rude blasts which the conflicts of Nations generate." Following the furor over the Seamen's bill, a growing number of Kentuckians came to share Clay's opinions.

By late February criticism of the Madison administration had swelled to such proportions in Kentucky that Governor Shelby felt it politic to excuse the outcry. To Secretary of State Monroe, who since the resignation of William Eustis in December had also been serving as acting secretary of war, Shelby wrote that recent events had had a "powerful and unpleasant effect" upon the Kentucky public. In a free nation, Shelby apologetically observed, "citizens will speak, write and act, often improperly from the want of correct *information,* and it is to be lamented that from that cause their censure too frequently attaches itself undeservedly to the supreme authority."

Whether Kentuckians were right or wrong in their criticisms of Madison, Shelby was apparently fully justified in expressing to Monroe his dread of "the consequences on the public mind of another abortive attempt to invade upper Canada on the West of Lake Erie." As the 1813 campaign season approached, waning confidence in the effectiveness of western armies composed largely of militia volunteers was evident in the numerous demands emanating from Kentucky for changes in the strategy and conduct of the campaign against Upper Canada. Calls were made for larger armies, greater federal support, and more regulars to bear the brunt of the fighting in the Northwest. At least one perceptive observer suggested, in a letter to the Lexington *Reporter,* that the invasion of Canada from the west should be abandoned entirely in favor of a concerted attack east of the Great Lakes.

On one aspect of the offensive against Upper Canada there was almost universal agreement in the state. Further land operations in the Northwest were deemed useless, unless the United States first gained naval command of Lake Erie. Recognizing the importance of this objective to revitalizing war spirit in the state, Shelby urged the Madison administration to take decisive steps to establish naval supremacy on the lake at the earliest possible moment. "It will have a good effect upon the public mind," he promised, "it will rouse their [Kentuckians'] hope and excite them to act from the apparent prospect of success crowning their labors."

That something was needed to spur recruiting in the state was evident. Lagging enthusiasm for a campaign that had produced many more casualties and far fewer victories than Kentuckians had anticipated was most vividly dramatized by the dwindling number of volunteers offering their services for the offensive in the Northwest. At the commencement of the war, eager Kentuckians had begged for an opportunity to participate in the invasion of Upper Canada. But in early 1813 a sufficient number of volunteers could not be obtained to fill the complement of 3,000 militiamen authorized by the General Assembly in the wake of the River Raisin debacle. Although Shelby insisted that "little reliance can be placed on Soldiers forced into the ranks," he was obliged to resort to a draft to raise the force.

Nor did Shelby find the recruits thus drafted into service of a quality comparable to those sent into the field in 1812. In March half the contingent of new levies was placed under the command of General Green Clay and ordered to the front in response to a request from Harrison for reinforcements. After inspecting one of the two regiments comprising Clay's command, Shelby regretfully informed Harrison that a "great part of them appeared to be men under size and in other respects hardly Kentuckians." The "better kind of people," Shelby complained, had hired substitutes. Under the circumstances, the disappointed governor asserted, no more volunteers could be expected from Kentucky until the federal government secured command of Lake Erie and authorized an army sufficiently large and well equipped to guarantee victory. Thwarted in their own local efforts to achieve their objectives in the war, Kentuckians were apparently looking to the federal government for more effective organization and direction of military operations in the Northwest.

But doubts that the federal government would take decisive steps to insure success in the Northwest continued to grow in the state. In March the *Kentucky Gazette* reported that Britain had opened the 1813 campaign by directing the Indians against settlements in the Indiana and Illinois territories. "Yet no preparation is made by the [federal] government to defend our territories!" the *Gazette* exclaimed. "Nor do we believe the executive intends any efficient succor for that quarter." Professing to believe that the Missouri, Illinois, and Indiana territories would soon be "overrun by the savages, desolated and ruined," the editor of the paper advised settlers and their families to flee to the Kentucky side of the Ohio River for safety.

The likelihood that the federal government would act with greater vigor to protect the frontiers and insure a successful invasion of Upper Canada was soon made to appear still more remote. News reached Kentucky in early April that Madison had accepted a Russian offer to mediate between the United States and Great Britain. To already skeptical Kentuckians, Madison's prompt acceptance of the Russian offer seemed clear proof that the president, like Congress, was more intent upon finding a way out of the war than upon injecting new energy into the American offensive against Canada.

The reaction in Kentucky to Madison's decision was indicative of the degree to which citizens of the state had become disenchanted with the nation's political leaders and with the prospects for victory under those leaders. It had been inconceivable to Kentuckians in mid-1812 that the war should end before the United States had ousted the British from Canada. But both the press and public in Kentucky were clearly divided in the spring of 1813 over the desirability of negotiating an end to the war before the United States had won a single significant victory.

The influential *Kentucky Gazette,* though highly critical of federal conduct of the war, was opposed to peace until the United States had proved its right to international respect upon the battlefield. "Can any man who has witnessed the *defeat* and *disgrace* thrown on our arms, the *treachery* of some of our officers and *citizens,* the base *sychophancy, corruption,* and *cowardice* of Congress, believe that the slightest prospect exists of an honorable peace with England, at the present moment?" the *Gazette* demanded. Despite Madison's many alleged failings, the editor of the *Gazette* could not believe that the president would sanction a peace that would mean the "disgrace and ruin of our country."

The widely read Lexington *Reporter,* however, came out strongly in favor of Russian mediation. The newspaper claimed that a large segment of the Kentucky public was prepared to accept a negotiated peace. The principal obstacle to peace in the minds of Kentuckians, the *Reporter* asserted, was the impressment issue. Reversing its earlier stand on the controversial Seamen's bill of February 1813, the *Reporter* now declared it a desirable measure which would greatly facilitate settlement of the impressment question.

A change in the editorial tactics of the *Kentucky Gazette* soon bore witness to the validity of the *Reporter's* claim of significant Kentucky support for a mediated peace. Assuming that sentiment in favor of Russian mediation was slight in the state, the *Gazette* first attempted to treat the proposal as a farce. In agreeing to the Russian offer, the *Gazette* explained, Madison had merely seized upon an opportunity to exile the administration's worst political enemies by appointing them peace commissioners. By early May, however, it was no longer possible for the editor of the newspaper to dismiss lightly the subject of peace talks as a farce. Instead the *Gazette* was reduced to imploring its wavering readers to avoid being "deluded with the foolish cry of peace" and to await the outcome of the projected negotiations before abandoning their support for the war.

With confidence in national leadership at a low ebb and opinion divided over the wisdom of continuing the war, some Kentuckians reasoned that only a resounding military victory could buoy flagging war spirit in the state. But during the spring and early summer of 1813 that victory failed to materialize. Indeed, another major defeat for Kentucky arms was soon added to the long series of discouraging reverses inflicted upon the United States during the first year of war.

Although the British forces commanded by General Henry Proctor had made no serious attempt during the remainder of the winter of 1813 to capitalize upon their victory at the River Raisin, a new British move was expected with the melting of the ice on Lake Erie. In the meantime, the expiration of many of his militia troops' periods of enlistment had drastically reduced the size of Harrison's Northwest Army. With scarcely 2,000 men remaining under his command and the spring campaigning season approaching, Harrison stood in desperate need of the reinforcements slowly organizing in Kentucky and Ohio.

Until he was adequately reinforced, Harrison could not hope to defend the entire Northwest frontier. He consequently reduced the commands stationed at most of the twelve forts and blockhouses under his authority to small garrison units. The bulk of his force, something over 1,000 men, he brought to Fort Meigs on the south bank of the Maumee River. There strenuous efforts were made to strengthen the fort's defenses in anticipation of the spring thaw and with it a possible British attack. Those preparations were largely complete, when on April 28 a long column of British troops swung into view before Fort Meigs.

Aware of Harrison's situation, Proctor was determined to crush Fort Meigs and capture its garrison before reinforcements could reach the post. To accomplish this, he had moved nearly 2,400 soldiers and Indians, together with heavy artillery and two gunboats, up the Maumee River from Lake Erie. Having spied out the ground beforehand, Proctor established his main batteries across the Maumee from Fort Meigs on the north bank. Later he placed smaller artillery pieces on the south side of the river below the fort.

For two days the British unloaded equipment and supplies from the gunboats, dug pits for their batteries, and made other careful preparations for a siege. While these preparations were going forward Indians under Tecumseh and Roundhead surrounded the fort, harassed its defenders, and drove away what livestock they could get their hands on. The guns of Fort Meigs responded only intermittently to this activity and interfered little with the progress of the British work parties. From behind the ramparts of the fort Harrison's artillerymen watched and waited, carefully hoarding their small supply of shot for the coming attack.

Their preparations finally completed, the British commenced a heavy bombardment of Fort Meigs on May 1. Roundshot and howitzer shells ploughed the escarpments of the earthen citadel and ripped away the roofs of its blockhouses. Twenty-four-pound balls flung great gouts of earth from atop the fort's underground magazines. Frantically, the defenders of Fort Meigs shoveled the dirt back into place to prevent balls heated red-hot by the British from exploding the stores of powder.

For four days the earthshaking, earsplitting pounding continued. American gunners, dueling sporadically with the British artillerists, could not match the weight of metal hurled at the beleaguered garrison. Altogether, more than 1,600 missiles rained down upon the shot-scarred fortress before the bombardment slackened. But American casualties were remarkably light, and Proctor's hopes of forcing the surrender of Fort Meigs before the garrison could be reinforced were doomed to disappointment. Shortly before midnight on May 4, a courier made his way into the besieged fort and delivered to Harrison a note from Brigadier General Green Clay. Clay's message stated that he and his 1,200 Kentuckians were proceeding down the Maumee in eighteen boats and were only two hours from Fort Meigs.

With reinforcements near at hand, Harrison quickly developed a plan for breaking the siege. A portion of Clay's approaching troops would be directed to capture and disable the main British batteries across the Maumee from Fort Meigs. Simultaneously a sortie would be made from the fort to attack the smaller batteries on the south side of the river. Precise instructions to Clay were drawn up and entrusted to Captain John Hamilton. The daring captain eluded the encircling Indians and reached Clay before dawn on May 5.

In accordance with his orders from Harrison, Clay divided his force and placed the 796 men in his twelve leading boats under the command of Lieutenant Colonel William Dudley. Dudley was directed to land his troops on the north bank of the Maumee, surprise the enemy batteries, and spike the captured guns. Having accomplished this task, he and his men were under specific orders to retreat immediately to their boats before the main body of British troops could counterattack. Clay, meanwhile, would land the men in the remaining six boats on the south bank above Fort Meigs and fight through the cordon of Indians to safety.

About nine o'clock the Kentuckians began their run down the river to Fort Meigs. Clay and the men of Colonel William Boswell's regiment failed to find the anticipated guides to direct them to their proper landing spot. In their confusion, Clay and Boswell crossed and recrossed the river before landing near the fort within range of the British artillery. With the element of surprise lost, their entry into the fort was opposed both by artillery fire and by swarming Indians. Harrison, however, ordered a sortie by the Pennsylvania Blues to relieve the battling Kentuckians, and Clay's contingent reached the gates with relatively light losses.

Across the river Dudley had already disembarked his men from their boats. In three columns the Kentuckians bore down upon the main British batteries. The left column circled behind the enemy artillery positions to prevent retreat. The center was held in reserve, while the right column, led by Dudley, swept over the lightly defended gun emplacements. To that point all had gone according to plan. The captured guns were quickly spiked, and Dudley was preparing to retreat to the boats and Fort Meigs. But his intentions were thwarted by the inexperience and lack of discipline so often characteristic of militia troops.

Looking across the field, Dudley realized for the first time that young Captain Leslie Combs, in command of the left column, had exceeded his instructions and was racing into imminent danger. Combs's column had not stopped as ordered after circling behind the captured batteries. Instead Combs was leading his men toward the main British camp with the obvious intention of attacking it. Though he had been warned that the British camp was too strong for his detachment to carry by storm, Dudley refused to abandon the men advancing to the attack. Ignoring or failing to observe Harrison's frantic signals from across the river, he rushed the remainder of his troops forward to support Combs's company.

Dudley's brave though unwise decision cost him his life. Having observed the capture of his batteries, Proctor hastily organized a force of British regulars and Canadian militia that met the charging Kentuckians head on. Indians from both sides of the river rushed in to join in the melee. With Dudley killed, with the British and Canadians pressing hard on their front, and with Indians swarming all around their flanks, the Kentuckians were soon thrown into confusion and overwhelmed. A small guard of 150 men assigned to defend the boats along the river-bank escaped. But the remainder of Dudley's detachment, close to 650 men, were either killed or captured.

As had happened at Frenchtown, the British allowed their Indian allies to get out of control following the pitched battle. The survivors of Dudley's defeat were quickly herded together by their British captors and marched away under a small guard of soldiers and Indians. Their destination was old Fort Miami, which Proctor was using as a base for supplies. As the dejected column of prisoners neared the fort more and more Indians appeared along the line of march. Despite the presence of British guards, the whooping Indians forced the Kentucky prisoners to run a guantlet of slashing knives and tomahawks to reach the interior of the old fort. Once inside, the Indians fell furiously upon the unarmed Kentuckians. A soldier of the British Forty-first attempted to intervene, but was struck down and killed. The carnage continued, although Proctor was himself reportedly on the scene by that time.

At least forty of the captured Kentuckians were slain before Tecumseh arrived and put an end to the bloodshed by threatening to kill any Indian who disobeyed his orders. Tecumseh is supposed to have vehemently reproached Proctor for his failure to stop the slaughter. When Proctor haughtily replied that the Indians were beyond control, Tecumseh is said to have shouted, "Begone! You are unfit to command; go and put on petticoats!"

While Dudley's detachment of Kentucky militiamen was being crushed and massacred on the north side of the Maumee, the second half of Harrison's plan was being carried out with greater success. On the south side of the river Colonel John Miller led 350 regulars and volunteers out of Fort Meigs and captured the British batteries below the fort with few losses. Among the men commanded by Miller was a company of Kentucky militia led by Captain Uriel Sebree. When the British position was overrun Sebree's company continued to drive the retreating British and Indians to a safe distance beyond the captured battery. Though counterattacked by four times their number, Sebree's men held the enemy at bay until Miller finished spiking the captured guns and sent forward reinforcements. For their conspicuous contribution to the success of the engagement Sebree and his Kentucky militia company were commended by Harrison in his official report of the May 5 engagements.

On neither side of the river, however, were the battles and sorties of May 5 decisive. Before the day was over the British had succeeded in removing the spikes from at least some of their recaptured guns and were again firing upon the fort. Had Proctor been able to keep his forces intact, the siege of Fort Meigs might have been resumed indefinitely. But he could not. With prisoners and captured supplies from Clay's and Dudley's boats to take home as booty, the Indians began to desert in large numbers. Proctor's Canadian militia soon began to insist that they, too, must return home to plant corn or face starvation in the fall. On May 9 Proctor abandoned the siege and retreated. But considering his losses during the siege, Harrison's position was little better than it had been before the arrival of the Kentucky reinforcements.

And in Kentucky the announcement of Dudley's defeat compounded the frustration and disillusionment already felt by much of the Kentucky public. Most of the assumptions with which Kentuckians had entered the war appeared to have been shattered beyond repair. Swift victories and military glory had eluded Kentucky volunteers. Instead they had suffered severe hardships, heavy losses, and deep humiliation. "The fate of war indeed falls heavily with its afflictions on KENTUCKY!" the *Kentucky Gazette* mourned in the aftermath of Dudley's defeat. Former United States Senator John Adair was also keenly conscious of the depths to which public morale had sunk. Upon returning to the state after an absence of several months, Adair sounded public opinion and wrote to Governor Shelby: "The Spirit of our countrymen, realy [sic] need something at this time to counteract the ill effect of repeated disasters."

But Shelby's "spirit" was, for the moment, no higher than that of his fellow citizens. Although he vigorously denied it, the "perturbed state" of his feelings was undoubtedly due in part to erroneous reports that his son James, a major in Dudley's regiment, was among those slain at Fort Meigs. Shelby would very shortly learn that his son was alive and returning home from the front. But in the meantime there were other reasons to account amply for the governor's despondent mood.

Shelby's energetic efforts to provide the men and to insure the conditions necessary to a successful campaign in the Northwest had failed to produce the victory Kentuckians had anticipated at the beginning of the war. Moreover, like many others in the state, Shelby had temporarily lost faith in the federal government's ability and willingness to prosecute the war effectively. "I am free to declare to you that as an individual, my Confidence in the Administration, especially as it relates to War Measures in the Western Country has greatly abated," Shelby confided to Henry Clay on May 16. "And I shall feel but little inclination in future," he continued, "to see a greater [sic] proportion of the best blood of Kentucky [than is required by law] put to hazard in the General cause in the War."

5

HEROES OF THE THAMES

THE PALL CAST UPON war spirit in Kentucky by the defeat of Dudley's regiment at Fort Meigs continued to hang like a dark cloud over the state through the spring and early summer of 1813. During these months, patriotic Kentuckians clutched at whatever straws of success were available in an effort to maintain their hopes for final victory.

Though American military operations on the Niagara front never achieved anything more decisive than a stalemate, the *Kentucky Gazette* pointed in mid-June to the capture of York and Fort George as evidence that the war was turning in favor of the United States. On the basis of the same indecisive victories, the Lexington *Reporter* declared the military outlook "optimistic" at the end of the first year of war. Similarly, Fourth of July orators in the state loudly proclaimed that isolated American victories at sea more than balanced American losses on land. And with more fervor than reason they predicted that the recent, minor successes along the Niagara border foreshadowed the complete conquest of Canada in the near future. Kentucky audiences responded to these orations with toasts and resolutions calling upon the federal government to provide the larger armies, higher taxes, and competent leadership Kentuckians had come to regard as essential to success on the battlefield.

But there was little indication that Fourth of July celebrants or others in Kentucky were prepared to make further sacrifices in the national cause until those demands had been met. In contrast to the two and one-half regiments raised in the state the preceding year, only one regiment of regulars, the Twenty-eighth Infantry, was recruited in Kentucky in 1813. Increased bounties offered by Congress for enlistment in this and other regiments created under the Act of January 29, 1813, apparently failed to offset Kentuckians' lagging enthusiasm for active service. Nor did a reduction in regular army enlistment periods from "five years or the duration of the war" to one year entice a sufficient number of Kentuckians into service to completely fill the ranks of the Twenty-eighth. Enlistments in the regiment fell short of authorized regimental strength by somewhere between 168 and 356 men.

The discouraging results of the first year of fighting also caused the number of Kentucky enlistments in militia and volunteer units to fall far below the totals for 1812. Governor Shelby, who had rejected offers of service from a surplus of eager volunteers in 1812, found it increasingly difficult to obtain volunteers for active service during the summer of 1813. The number of troops of all descriptions sent into the field by Kentucky in the first seven months of 1813 was only about half the total number provided during the six months of war the preceding year. It was the latter half of the summer before a combination of seemingly favorable events revived real hope for military successes and restored a measure of the initial enthusiasm Kentuckians had felt for the War of 1812.

No one was more keenly aware than Isaac Shelby of the low state of public morale in Kentucky in the spring and early summer of 1813. Nevertheless, Shelby believed that Kentuckians would again take the field in large numbers if promised an opportunity to fight in a manner and for an objective which suited their inclinations. Despite personal misgivings about the effectiveness of

American leadership in the war, the governor made a new appeal on July 31 for volunteers to reinforce Harrison's Northwest Army. This appeal was masterfully contrived to overcome Kentuckians' objections to further service in the Northwest.

Though uncertain himself how many militia troops the War Department would accept into federal service, Shelby assured prospective volunteers that the government had finally authorized a force sufficiently large to act effectively against Upper Canada. The campaign, Shelby asserted, would be brief; no one's services would be required for more than sixty days after arriving at headquarters. The prospects for success were depicted as high. "Now is the time to act," the governor's proclamation declared, "and by one decisive blow, put an end to the contest in that quarter." Cognizant of Kentuckians' distaste for service as foot soldiers, Shelby called only for mounted riflemen. And as a guarantee of reliable leadership, Shelby, the venerated hero of King's Mountain, promised to lead the volunteers to Canada in person.

Pleased with the initial reaction to his proclamation, Shelby was at first highly confident that "the prospect of acting efficiently against Upper Canada" would revive enthusiasm for the war in Kentucky. In a letter to Harrison on August 4 he predicted that "four or five thousand volunteers and perhaps a much larger number" would assemble at Newport on August 31, the appointed day of rendezvous. His confidence seemed justified. Newspapers in the Bluegrass area reported a rash of enlistments following publication of the governor's appeal for volunteers. Public spirit appeared to be aroused to a high pitch, and at every hand Shelby heard forecasts that "five Thousand men & probably a much greater number" would turn out to march with him to Canada.

Yet the wave of excitement which swept the state soon subsided. By August 8, Shelby was far less certain of the response his appeal would evoke and scaled his estimate down to two to three thousand volunteers. In a more cautious mood, he again wrote to Harrison. "You were not mistaken," he informed the general, "as to the indisposition of the people here to turn out again & it has taken great exertion to reanimate them." He warned Harrison that careful arrangements should be made to supply the expedition adequately on its march to the front. For, Shelby declared, if lack of provisions "or any other trifling occurrence should disgust the volunteers . . . rest assured that there will be an end to the spirit of volunteering from Kentucky."

Several days later Shelby was still more perturbed by the failure of Kentuckians to step forward in the numbers he had at first expected. Disenchantment with the war was greater in the state than Shelby had divined, and he confessed himself "greatly mortified" by the discovery. Enlistments from the area south of the Kentucky River were particularly disappointing. To Harrison, Shelby reported that he had been forced to order a draft of 1,500 men from that region.

Enthusiasm for the projected expedition was more heartening north of the Kentucky River. But even there Shelby now hoped for no more than 1,000 volunteers. Forgetting the depths to which his own zeal for the war had sunk earlier in the year, Shelby wrote on August 11: "I never have been so far disappointed in the patriotism of my countrymen, before, & am at a loss to what cause to attribute their backwardness all at once."

Despite Shelby's glum appraisal of the situation in early August, his plan to lead an expedition to Canada prepared the way for a major improvement in public morale. Many Kentuckians, their pride stung by the earlier defeats inflicted upon the United States, wanted to believe that a swift strike into Canada might yet be successful. Moreover, faith in Shelby's abilities as a military commander was widespread in the state. Upon receipt of the news of Dudley's defeat, the General Assembly had unhesitatingly turned to Shelby with a unique request that the governor take personal charge of Ken-

tucky troops in the Northwest theater. And in the belief
that confidence in Shelby's military talents would greatly
inspire Kentucky volunteers, Harrison also urged Shelby
to join him at the front.

While not immediately apparent, the timing of
Shelby's call for volunteers to participate in a decisive
campaign in the Northwest also fortunately corresponded
with political and military events outside the state.
Doubts about the federal government's determination to
wage vigorous war against Britain had by 1813 become
one of the greatest deterrents to voluntary enlistments
from Kentucky. At the very time that Shelby's appeal was
issued, however, the Thirteenth Congress was in the
process of adopting new measures to fund the war more
adequately through the end of the year. The new funding
legislation included duties on a variety of domestic and
imported products, a direct tax of $3 million to be appor-
tioned among the states, and authorization to borrow $7.5
million to meet anticipated war costs. News of the recently enacted war legislation was reported in Kentucky
within days of Shelby's order to draft recruits from south
of the Kentucky River for the expedition to Canada. To
Kentuckians, the news accounts were encouraging evidence of returning congressional vigor.

Public morale in the state was further boosted by simul-
taneous reports that Madison had also requested from
Congress an embargo on American shipping. At Max-
well's Spring on the Fourth of July, a large crowd of
Lexingtonians supported Madison's request with the
toast: "Our Mechanics and Manufacturers—Who keep
our wealth at home, and would make us independent of
the world; let Congress protect their interests." Similar
expressions of sentiment at other celebrations in the state
were indicative of the importance Kentuckians had come
to attach to embargoes as a mechanism for diverting
American investment capital from shipping to manufacturing enterprises. The strength of their feelings
stemmed from a belief that the United States could never

achieve real economic independence from England so long as American farmers were dependent upon British markets and manufactured goods.

From a tactical standpoint, too, Kentuckians regarded an embargo as a highly desirable wartime measure. Illicit American trafficking with the enemy was believed by Kentuckians to be widespread and was bitterly resented in the state. The British would have been unable to defend Canada, Kentuckians argued, were it not for provisions which reached them from the United States. New Englanders, especially, were accused of feeding the British, "when they are at our very doors, murdering, plundering, and burning." The profits reaped from illegal trade with the enemy by influential shippers, Kentuckians believed, were largely responsible for the deplorable neutral stance adopted during the war by government officials in Massachusetts and some other New England states. The most effective means of controlling smuggling activities, it was argued, was an embargo on all exports.

Kentuckians were greatly disappointed when, on August 10, they learned that the embargo requested by Madison had been defeated by two votes in the United States Senate. Leading newspapers in the state joined in roundly denouncing the Senate for rejecting "the wisest and most important measure introduced during the session." Nevertheless, Kentuckians were generally heartened on the eve of the Shelby expedition's departure for Canada by the overall record of the Thirteenth Congress. The revenue measures enacted by Congress were accepted as a pledge that the war would be continued with new energy and determination. At the same time Madison's request for an embargo on American shipping, even though defeated, inspired fresh confidence in presidential leadership among citizens of the state.

Heartening news of a dramatic American military victory in northern Ohio also reached Kentucky in mid-August and further lifted Kentuckians' spirits in the final weeks before Shelby's projected invasion of Canada. Following the siege of Fort Meigs, William Henry Harrison had moved his headquarters to Upper Sandusky and to Cleveland, where he began raising troops and provisions for a renewed offensive against Upper Canada. By late July, 800 untrained recruits and most of Harrison's supplies for the rebuilding Northwest Army were lying near Upper Sandusky at an unfortified position only thirty miles up the Sandusky River from Lake Erie. Harrison's position on the Sandusky was an extremely vulnerable one when Proctor, with about 1,400 British, Canadians, and Indians, again struck at American defenses in the Northwest.

Moving his British and Canadian troops by boat along the shores of Lake Erie, Proctor first ascended the Maumee River to test again the defenses of Fort Meigs. But Fort Meigs, commanded by General Green Clay in Harrison's absence, was better provisioned and more heavily manned when the British appeared on July 20 than it had been on the occasion of the first siege. With no field pieces larger than six-pounders at his disposal, Proctor knew that he could neither pound the American garrison into submission nor carry the post by storm. His only chance for success lay in drawing the American garrison from the fort and into an ambush. After several days of desultory artillery fire, a ruse devised by Tecumseh was attempted. In the woods beyond sight of the fort, Tecumseh's warriors acted out a sham battle in hopes of luring the defenders of Fort Meigs to the aid of an imaginary American relief column. The banging of muskets and the Indian war whoops emanating from the woods might have been convincing, had Clay not already received word from Harrison that he could expect no reinforcements. The British ruse thus failed, and on July 28 Proctor's army abandoned the siege and departed.

Having failed to accomplish anything before Fort Meigs, Proctor was desperate for a victory. His best opportunity appeared to lie in an attack upon Harrison's unfortified base in northern Ohio. By routing the 800 raw militia recruits and seizing the stores painstakingly gathered by Harrison at Upper Sandusky, the British commander could strike a crippling blow at American plans for a renewed offensive against Detroit and Malden. As Proctor's seemingly overwhelming forces approached the mouth of the Sandusky River in late July, all that stood between them and their objective was tiny Fort Stephenson.

A small, stockaded, frontier outpost, Fort Stephenson stood at Lower Sandusky, only ten miles upriver from Lake Erie. Twenty-two-year-old Major George Croghan, a Kentuckian and an officer of the Seventeenth United States Infantry, commanded the little fort. His position was not an enviable one. Croghan's entire garrison consisted of only 160 regulars, with which to oppose the advance of an enemy force nearly 1,400 strong. His only artillery was a single six-pounder, affectionately known as "Old Bess." And the fort that he commanded boasted nothing stronger than timber pickets as protection against the enemy's cannon. So convinced was Harrison that the post was untenable, that he ordered Croghan on July 29 to burn Fort Stephenson and withdraw toward Upper Sandusky.

Croghan, however, was reluctant to obey. In response to Harrison's orders, he wrote: "We have determined to maintain this place, and by Heaven, we will." The next day Croghan appeared at Harrison's headquarters personally to plead for an opportunity to defend Fort Stephenson. Though outraged by the young major's rebellious reluctance to obey orders, Harrison finally succumbed to Croghan's earnest entreaties and amended his original orders. The order to burn Fort Stephenson was rescinded, and Croghan was permitted to retain command of the post. His new instructions were to retreat at the approach of a British force if time permitted. That Croghan disdained to do when Proctor's British and Indians appeared before Fort Stephenson on August 1.

Massacre of captured Kentuckians at Frenchtown following the battle at the River Raisin
Courtesy of Clements Library, University of Michigan

Tecumseh halts the
slaughter of Kentuckians
captured in Dudley's
Defeat at Fort Meigs
*Courtesy of Indiana
Historical Society Library*

Richard M. Johnson slays Tecumseh in the Battle of the Thames
Courtesy of the Library of Congress

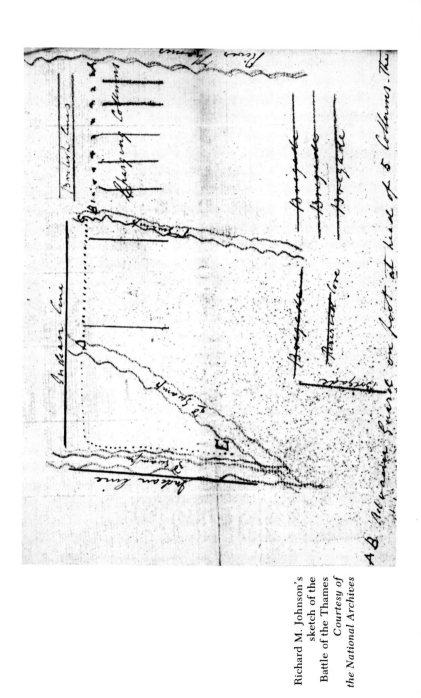

Richard M. Johnson's
sketch of the
Battle of the Thames
*Courtesy of
the National Archives*

Though vastly outnumbered, Croghan curtly rejected a British demand to surrender and scorned the threat of an Indian massacre should he be defeated. That night and through most of the following day, Croghan and the men of his command stoically endured an intermittent bombardment by Proctor's gunboats and shore batteries. Fortunately for the defenders of Fort Stephenson, the British field howitzers were too light to breach the walls of the fort. The scarred and splintered pickets were still intact when, late in the afternoon of August 2, Proctor ended the bombardment and ordered a direct assault on the fort.

From behind the wooden walls of Fort Stephenson, Croghan watched calmly as British regulars of the Forty-first Regiment, supported by militia and Indians, advanced in three columns to the attack. Having anticipated a thrust against the northwest angle of the stockade, Croghan had already positioned his one artillery piece to bear directly upon the protecting ditch surrounding the fort. "Old Bess," loaded with grapeshot, ripped the orderly British columns to shreds as they emerged from the smoke of their own weapons and poured into the ditch below the walls. American rifle fire, withheld at Croghan's orders until the last moment, scattered the swarming Indian warriors at the first volley and wreaked havoc among the closely packed British ranks.

For two hours the gallant regulars of the British Forty-first withstood the withering American fire and continued to batter at the unyielding walls of Fort Stephenson. Finally, with every officer dead and fully one-fifth of their number killed, wounded, or captured, the Forty-first was recalled. During the two days of siege and assault only one American had been killed and seven wounded. Despite the best efforts of Proctor's most reliable troops, the American flag still flew defiantly over Fort Stephenson. Unwilling to continue the costly attack and hesitant to move south against Harrison with the defenders of Fort Stephenson at his back, Proctor ordered his troops to their transports and began a retreat to Malden.

Croghan's defense of Fort Stephenson was possibly the most celebrated instance of individual heroism by a Kentuckian during the War of 1812. Coming at a period in the war when American fortunes were at a low ebb and American morale badly in need of a lift, Croghan's refusal to abandon the lonely wilderness outpost in the face of seemingly overwhelming odds fired the public imagination. Throughout the country Croghan's heroism was praised by orators and journalists. In his official report of the battle William Henry Harrison wrote: "It will not be among the least of General Proctor's mortifications to find that he has been baffled by a youth, who has just passed his twenty-first year. He is, however, a hero worthy of his gallant uncle, General George R. Clarke [*sic*]." Upon receiving this report, President Madison immediately elevated the youthful Croghan from the rank of major to the brevet rank of lieutenant colonel. Years later, when it was pointed out to Andrew Jackson that Croghan's promising career had been blighted by intemperance, the outspoken hero of New Orleans replied that in his opinion Croghan's brilliant defense of Fort Stephenson entitled the man "to be drunk for the rest of his life." Congress apparently agreed, for in 1835 the national legislature presented a gold medal to George Croghan and swords to each of his officers in memory of the stirring repulse of Proctor's army at Fort Stephenson.

In Kentucky jubilation over Croghan's victory combined with elation over the recently enacted federal war measures to stimulate recruiting for the Shelby expedition against Upper Canada. During the last two weeks of August voluntary enlistments rose dramatically in the state. The *Kentucky Gazette* reported three new companies of mounted volunteers raised in Fayette County during that period. At Frankfort the *Argus* announced that a sudden rush of volunteers had swelled the ranks of a regiment being raised there to nearly double their original number. "We have [also] heard in the course of the present week," the *Argus* declared on August 22,

1813, "from various parts of the state, and have much pleasure in stating, that the spirit of Volunteering is very great." Before the end of the month Shelby had a sufficient number of volunteers for the expedition to justify rescinding his August 11 order for a draft.

Shelby arrived at Newport on August 31 to find 3,500 mounted volunteers prepared to take the field with him. Had the departure of the expedition been delayed until mid-September, the force Shelby led to the front would undoubtedly have been still larger. For Oliver Hazard Perry's September 10 victory over the British fleet on Lake Erie raised war sentiment in Kentucky to its highest pitch since the declaration of hostilities. In towns and counties throughout the state Perry's victory was celebrated with "parades, illuminations, etc." And justly so. By achieving naval superiority on Lake Erie, Perry rendered further British offensives in the American Northwest impossible and left Upper Canada extremely vulnerable to attack. Fully aware of this, Kentuckians were eager to see the advantage pressed and the conquest of Upper Canada finally accomplished.

Not even reports of a new threat to states and territories in the American Southwest could dampen Kentuckians' rekindled ardor for war in September 1813. Reports that Creek Indians had massacred both settlers and soldiers at Fort Mims in Alabama served only to whet expanding Kentucky appetites for tangible gains to offset earlier American losses in the war. Upon receiving the reports, the *Kentucky Gazette* immediately charged British and Spanish agents at Pensacola with instigating the Creek attack. Americans, the editor suggested, should welcome the Indian war as an excuse to seize the Floridas from Spain.

No suggestion was made, however, that Kentucky should send troops to participate in the war in the Southwest. Perry's victory had breathed new life into the concept of regional responsibility for military campaigns in the various theaters of war. And Kentuckians continued to regard their own realm of military responsibility as limited to the Northwest. Militia forces from Tennessee, Georgia, and Mississippi Territory were expected to defend the Southwest and to carry the war into the Floridas. In Kentucky attention remained riveted upon the campaign against Upper Canada.

Events were moving swiftly toward a climax in the Northwest. William Henry Harrison had awaited news of the Battle of Lake Erie at his headquarters on the Sandusky River in northern Ohio. The anxiously awaited report from Perry reached him on September 12. "We have met the enemy, and they are ours," Perry wrote. The following day Harrison established a new headquarters on the shore of Lake Erie near the Portage River. With him was a seasoned force of nearly 1,000 mounted Kentucky volunteers raised and commanded by Congressman Richard M. Johnson. From Upper Sandusky and from Fort Meigs small units of regulars under Brigadier Generals Lewis Cass and Duncan McArthur were in motion toward the new camp. Governor Shelby, having pushed his 3,500 mounted Kentuckians rapidly north from Newport, was only two days' ride from Lake Erie.

By September 20 all of the gathering forces had converged upon Harrison's headquarters. At least 5,000 troops, most of them Kentucky volunteers, stood ready to attempt the invasion of Upper Canada. Harrison moved his troops against Detroit and Malden by two routes. Johnson's mounted regiment was ordered to march overland and rejoin the main body near the Detroit River. The remainder of the invasion force embarked on Perry's ships, and on September 27 they landed on the Canadian shore within a few miles of Fort Malden.

To oppose the American invasion Proctor had at Detroit and Malden nearly 1,000 British regulars. With him, too, were Tecumseh and between 3,000 and 3,500 Indian warriors. But Proctor, fearful of being cut off from his bases of supply on Lake Ontario, had no intention of defending either post. As the Americans approached he abandoned the forts, and with possibly a third of Tecumseh's Indians accompanying his troops, began a leisurely retreat eastward along the Thames River.

Leaving sizable detachments to guard his bases on the Canadian shore and to garrison Detroit, Harrison took up the pursuit on October 2 with slightly over 3,000 men. His force consisted of Johnson's mounted regiment, Shelby's volunteers, and a small contingent of 120 regulars. By October 4 the hotly pursuing Kentuckians were pressing hard upon the rear elements of Proctor's army and threatening to turn retreat into rout. On October 5 they came up with the main body of British and Indians.

The harried British had chosen to make their final stand in a wooded area a mile or two from Moraviantown. When the oncoming Kentucky volunteers burst upon the narrow field, they discovered the British regulars formed in two double lines across their path. A small swamp, impassable to both infantry and horse, divided the British left from the British right. From the swampy area in the center the British left extended to the Thames River. On the other side their right extended to a larger, densely grown swamp that ran forward at an angle toward Harrison's approaching army. Tecumseh and his warriors lay hidden in this swamp, waiting to pour their fire into the Kentuckians' left flank as they advanced against the British.

Harrison wasted no time before moving his troops into order of battle. Observing that the waiting British were formed in open rather than closed ranks, he decided upon the unorthodox plan of holding Shelby's dismounted troops in reserve and sending Johnson's mounted regiment against the enemy. "The American backwoodsmen," Harrison later wrote of Johnson's Kentuckians, "ride better in woods than any other people." His decision was also based upon a conviction that the British, sheltered behind trees in expectation of an infantry attack, "would be quite unprepared for the shock [of a cavalry charge], and that they could not resist it."

Harrison's arrangements for the attack were quickly carried out. Three brigades of Kentucky militia under Major General William Henry were drawn up in parallel lines facing the British. The remainder of the reserve, commanded by General Joseph Desha, were drawn up in lines facing the large swamp on the American left. Shelby, with his aide General John Adair, stationed himself at the critical angle where Desha's right joined Henry's left.

Johnson, in the interim, had divided his regiment in order to attack Proctor's regulars on both sides of the small swamp stretching through the center of the British line. When the bugle sounded the charge, his brother, Lieutenant Colonel James Johnson, led one battalion forward along the Thames riverbank against the British left. With the other battalion, Johnson angled across the battlefield to fall upon the British right.

Skillfully weaving their way through the trees, the mounted Kentuckians nearest the river ripped through the first line of British regulars and bore down upon the second. Firing from the saddle, they fought their way through the second line of regulars with equal ease. Ten minutes after the charge was sounded the fighting on the British left was over. The half of Johnson's regiment commanded by his brother was behind the British lines. Fanning out to form a loose net, the victorious Kentuckians captured scores of retreating British soldiers seeking to escape to Moraviantown.

Crashing through the light undergrowth on the opposite side of the field, Richard M. Johnson's battalion also routed the regulars on the British right. But Johnson's command came under a galling fire from Indian marksmen lurking in the large swamp on their left flank. Unable to force their horses through the thick brush and marshy ground where the Indians lay, Johnson's men were forced to dismount and continue the fight on foot.

It was obvious to all that the nature of the ground would make it particularly difficult to dislodge the determined

Indians from their well-protected positions. Johnson was also fearful that a general charge upon the dense swamp would result in extraordinarily heavy casualties. To lessen the number of casualties he resorted to a desperate tactic. Regrouping his men, he called for twenty volunteers to make the initial rush upon the swamp. Their task was to draw the first fire from the hundreds of warriors hidden in the heavy undergrowth and permit the main body to close before the Indians could reload. For the twenty men who volunteered death was nearly certain.

Command of the famed "Forlorn Hope" was given to William Whitley, a sixty-three-year-old pioneer settler of Lincoln County, Kentucky. Johnson, conspicuously mounted on a white mare, charged with the little company of dismounted volunteers to the very edge of the Indian-infested swamp. Hundreds of musket balls shredded the air around the charging men and tore at their clothing and bodies. Fifteen of the heroic band, including Whitley, were killed immediately by the withering fire from the hidden warriors; four others were wounded. Only one man escaped unhurt.

Richard M. Johnson was twice wounded. Shot through the hip and the thigh, he nevertheless retained his seat on the white mare and continued in the thick of the hand-to-hand fighting that followed. Shelby sent a portion of the reserve forward under Lieutenant Colonel James Simrall to assist in the final rush upon the Indian position. Slowly, the knife-wielding, tomahawk-carrying Kentuckians pushed the outnumbered warriors from the swamp and forced them to flee.

Before the hotly contested engagement ended, Johnson received three more wounds and, in personal combat, killed an Indian chieftain supposed to have been Tecumseh. Without question Tecumseh died in the fray and with him died Indian hopes of holding back the tide of settlement pushing into the Northwest Territories. Whether or not the Indian dispatched by Johnson was in fact Tecumseh, the legend persisted. In 1836 grateful citizens from all parts of the nation supported Johnson's successful bid for the vice-presidency of the United States with the chant:

> *Rumpsey-dumpsey, rumpsey-dumpsey,*
> *Colonel Johnson killed Tecumseh.*

The army with which Proctor and his predecessors had captured Detroit and harassed the American Northwest was completely destroyed in the Battle of the Thames. Proctor's Indian allies were dispersed and many soon sued for peace. Only twelve British soldiers were killed and twenty-two wounded, but more than 600 British prisoners were taken by the victorious Kentuckians. All of the defeated army's artillery, stores, and powder also fell into American hands.

There was great rejoicing in Harrison's camp when it was discovered that the captured artillery included three pieces taken from Burgoyne in 1777 and recaptured by the British at Detroit. But the knowledge that they had retaken all but one of the battle flags captured by the British at Detroit, the River Raisin, and in Dudley's Defeat was particularly satisfying to the Kentucky volunteers. That Kentucky's record in the War of 1812 was pointed to by numerous eastern journals as a lesson in patriotism and military ardor for other states to emulate was due more to the services and sacrifices of Kentucky volunteer soldiers than to the achievements of regular officers like George Croghan and Zachary Taylor. And at the Battle of the Thames the Kentucky citizen-soldier avenged earlier humiliations and enjoyed his finest hour.

6

A WAR FOR
NATIONAL SURVIVAL

For Kentucky and the Northwest the victory at the Thames was of enormous importance. Its most important consequence was permanently to reestablish the American frontier on the Detroit River. But the temporary control that it brought over a portion of Canadian territory was also significant. Command of both shores of Lake Erie prevented a resurgence of British power on the lake and in Upper Canada. It ended the threat of a renewed British attack upon American territories north of the Ohio River and left Tecumseh's Indian confederation not only leaderless but also isolated from its source of supplies and munitions. As a result the barrier to American settlement in the Northwest was considerably reduced.

There was particular satisfaction for Kentuckians in the victory at the Thames for other reasons as well. The victory accomplished the principal military goals that citizens of the state had set for themselves at the beginning of the war and seemed to vindicate many of their concepts of military strategy. Prior to the declaration of war Kentuckians in Congress and at home had strongly supported the United States' traditional reliance upon militia rather than standing armies. Though the series of American defeats in the Northwest had prompted numerous appeals from the state in early 1813 for larger regular armies, the determination with which volunteer troops routed the British and Indians at the Thames temporarily rejuvenated Kentuckians' original faith in the effectiveness of the citizen-soldier. In addition, the rapidity with which Upper Canada was conquered following Perry's victory on Lake Erie was regarded as adequate vindication for Kentuckians' insistence during the spring and summer of 1813 that the federal government take steps to secure command of the lake before continuing the offensive in the Northwest.

Upon Kentuckians' attitudes toward American war aims the victory at the Thames had an opposite effect. Before war was declared Kentucky War Hawks had argued that the United States was being forced into hostilities to preserve its independence against British infringements on national rights. They vehemently denied every implication that the purpose of the war was to acquire territory from Great Britain. But in late 1813 elation over the success of Shelby's expedition caused many Kentucky spokesmen to succumb to the temptation to make territorial aggrandizement a principal object of the war. News of the victory prompted an immediate cry in the state for the retention of Upper Canada and any other British territory held by the United States when peace was concluded.

Distinctly sectional interests had little to do with this suddenly aroused thirst for additional territory. The Kentucky demand for territorial acquisitions extended beyond the retention of Upper Canada to the annexation of other territories in which Kentuckians had little or no direct sectional interest. The upsurge of expansive nationalism awakened in the state by the victory at the Thames had from the beginning prompted cries for Lower as well as Upper Canada. And when reports reached the state in November 1813 that Andrew Jackson's Tennessee volunteers had won a series of engagements against the Creeks and were preparing to push into Spanish Florida, equally fervent territorial ambitions were aroused in that direction. Kentucky expansionists quickly coupled cries for the annexation of Florida with demands for all of Canada.

For Kentuckians the months following the victory at the Thames were the brightest period of the war. To the triumph in Canada and the anticipated conquest of Florida there was added a victory in Congress. Sentiment in favor of an embargo to promote American manufactures and put an end to illicit trade with the enemy in Canada had steadily intensified in the state during the fall of 1813. Great hostility continued to be manifested toward the United States Senate for its failure to adopt the embargo proposed by Madison the previous July. Some Kentuckians became so bitter against the Senate that they openly advocated "*reducing* the term of service in that truly *independent* body" in order to make it more amenable to popular control.

Thus when Congress, in compliance with a second request from Madison, reversed itself and on December 17 passed an embargo act, many Kentuckians welcomed it with as much enthusiasm as they had the victory at the Thames. Though many newspapers in the state joined in approving the event, none was more jubilant than the *Kentucky Gazette*. "Fellow citizens," the *Gazette* proclaimed, "if ever you had just occasion of rejoicing since the commencement of the war, this is the moment—the *Embargo* will effect more than your most skillful generals & best appointed army can, whilst to the end of time its passage will be considered as the triumph of American republicanism." At public dinners, at rallies, and in letters to local newspapers Kentucky voters were similarly extravagant in their approbation of the new legislation. Those Kentucky representatives who had supported the embargo bill were lavishly praised by their constituents. The three Kentucky congressmen who had opposed the measure—Samuel McKee, William P. Duvall, and Thomas Montgomery—were subjected to equally lavish abuse. Of the three, only McKee succeeded in retaining his seat in the congressional elections of the following year.

With the British defeated in the Lake Erie region, with an embargo enacted into legislation, and with optimistic reports reaching the state from the Southwest theater, many Kentuckians were encouraged in late 1813 to believe that complete victory over England was imminent. Although setbacks on Canadian soil at the Chateaugay River and at Chrysler's Farm in late October and November 1813 stymied American attempts to assault Montreal before the end of the year, these were regarded as only temporary reverses and did little to suppress soaring Kentucky hopes. Decisive battles for control of Lakes Ontario and Champlain were anticipated with the resumption of campaigning in the early spring, and confidence was high in the state that American victories on the lakes would open the way for a successful assault upon Lower Canada.

Confidence that complete victory was within the grasp of the United States was significantly heightened in Kentucky by Madison's announcement, in January 1814, that Great Britain had proposed direct peace negotiations with the United States. The timing of the British proposal seemed highly significant to some Kentucky observers. They strongly suggested that the British government, in making its offer to negotiate, was motivated by fear of impending defeat. On the assumption that Britain's forces in Canada were growing proportionately weaker as American forces strengthened with time and experience, the *Kentucky Gazette* characterized the proposed negotiations as a stratagem intended to divert congressional attention from preparations for an irresistible spring offensive. The only object of the British proposal, the *Gazette* emphatically declared, is *"to unnerve the energies of our government."*

The controversy that arose in the state over Madison's decision to accept the British proposal was a direct reflection of the heightened confidence with which Kentuckians viewed American prospects for complete victory in late 1813 and early 1814. Although Kentuckians heartily approved Madison's selection of Henry Clay as one of the American peace commissioners, there was strong opposition in the state to negotiating an early end to the conflict. Both proponents and opponents of a negotiated end to the war assumed that Britain was prepared to grant the United States satisfaction on the maritime issues in dispute between the two nations. The core of the controversy was whether the United States should content itself with limited territorial gains from the war. Those who supported Madison's decision to negotiate directly with Britain were prepared to end the war with satisfaction on the maritime issues, retention of Upper Canada, and annexation of whatever portion of Florida could be conquered before a treaty was concluded. Opponents of an early end to the war wanted to continue the conflict until the conquest of Canada and the Floridas was completed.

In the debate expectations of further conquests appear to have overridden concern over the effects of continuing the costly struggle. The most influential voice raised in favor of a negotiated end to the war was that of the Lexington *Reporter*. The equally influential *Kentucky Gazette,* however, was even more vociferous in demanding that the offensive against Canada be continued. The General Assembly lent official weight to this demand by resolving on February 1 in favor of "a vigorous, energetic and zealous prosecution of the war." And at the February celebrations of Washington's Birthday annually held in various towns and counties, numerous private citizens expressed their desire for the conquest of all of Florida and Canada. The only acceptable peace, celebrants at Lexington proclaimed, would be a "peace negotiated with Great Britain under the auspices of the American eagle, firmly perched on the towers of Quebec."

For several reasons such exuberant expectations of complete victory in the war proved to be short-lived. In the early months of 1814 American efforts failed to achieve naval dominance on Lake Ontario and Lake Champlain. Kentucky observers correctly perceived that, lacking control of the lakes, the contemplated American offensive of 1814 was foredoomed to failure. Faith in the Madison administration's ability effectively to prosecute the war again plummeted in the state. Governor Shelby was particularly discouraged by the military situation and by the continuing opposition of New England Federalists to the war. Privately he concluded that peace, on whatever terms could be arranged, might be preferable to prolonging the conflict. "Perhaps it will be well for us if we do obtain peace," Shelby wrote John J. Crittenden in April 1814. "The war is a ruinous one—We are literally a house divided against itself. And although we may not fall the war if carried on will finally exhaust the best blood and interest of the Nation."

Kentucky hopes for complete victory in the war were further dimmed when it was learned in April that Congress, at Madison's request, had repealed the Embargo Act passed the preceding December. Outraged by the president's action, Kentuckians vehemently denounced both Madison and Congress. Having relinquished a valuable and effective weapon, they argued, the United States could expect the British government to increase its demands at the peace table. Already, Congressman Joseph Desha reported from Washington shortly after the vote on repeal, rumors were circulating that a peace treaty would soon be concluded. It was further rumored, Desha wrote, that Canada would not be mentioned in the treaty and that the treaty would suspend only the practice of impressment while leaving other maritime issues to be settled in subsequent negotiations.

The greatest blow to Kentuckians' hopes for further military conquests came in June, with reports that Napoleon Bonaparte had abdicated his throne and that France was defeated. The news immediately changed the whole complexion of the war between the United States and Great Britain. Freed from the war in Europe, the British government could concentrate all its forces against the United States. "There is now no barrier between our country and our deadly enemy, the British," the *Kentucky Gazette* declared. Negotiations for peace were also doomed, the Lexington *Reporter* predicted, unless Americans were prepared to surrender on impressment and other issues affecting the sovereignty of the United States. The future for the United States, both newspapers agreed, was "bleak." Americans were the only people still at war with the world's mightiest nation.

The brief period during which Kentuckians had succumbed to the temptation to make territorial gains an object of war came to an end. The moment British reinforcements arrived from Europe, they now insisted, American efforts to conquer Canada would have to be abandoned. Domestic discord would have to cease in the United States; Americans would have to unite in defending the nation's borders against the anticipated British onslaught. The war, Kentuckians warned, had ceased to be a contest for either territorial gain or for the maintenance of maritime rights. It had become a war for national survival.

The drastic alteration effected in Britain's military potential in America by the defeat of Napoleon also caused a major change in the attitude of the Kentucky public toward the conduct of the war. Popular proposals for countering the anticipated buildup of British forces in America placed a new emphasis on centralized direction of the American war effort. The reliance Kentuckians had placed upon highly decentralized military operations at the commencement of the struggle was correspondingly diminished. In what they believed to be an hour of impending crisis, Kentuckians turned to the federal government for effective leadership. Madison was called upon to rid his cabinet of weak advisers, and Congress was exhorted to act with vigor and determination regardless of political or economic costs.

Through their newspapers and political representatives, concerned Kentuckians repeatedly suggested numerous military preparations that they had come to regard as essential. The size of the regular army, they insisted, should be greatly increased. To insure more effective military leadership, the practice of promoting officers on the basis of merit rather than seniority should be instituted. Adoption of a uniform, national militia code to improve the performance of the nation's militia forces was also considered highly important. To further improve the militia force it was frequently suggested that all volunteers be required to serve for the duration of the war, or for a period of at least two years. And to support the expanded military organization Congress was urged to double federal taxes. In effect, Kentuckians were demanding that the federal government reduce its dependence upon the states and assume a larger share of responsibility for both the size and quality of American military forces.

The federal government's failure or inability to meet these demands soon brought the Madison administration under increasingly sharp attack in the state. Criticism became severe when, in July 1814, an American offensive on the Niagara front failed to sweep the British from the northern shores of Lake Ontario. After winning a hard-fought victory at Chippewa, the American army under General Jacob Brown was checked at Lundy's Lane and forced to retire to the Niagara River. Kentuckians attributed the repulse of Brown's attempted invasion primarily to lack of effective support from the United States' Lake Ontario fleet. And they held Madison chiefly responsible for the fleet's inactivity, on the theory that he had consistently failed to provide the means necessary to establish naval dominance on the lake.

Criticisms of Madison reached their peak in Kentucky in early September, following news of the first major offensive blow struck by Britain against the United States. For some months British naval units had been operating along the Atlantic coast, harrying American shipping and terrorizing the coastal population. On August 18 the largest of the British fleets in American waters ascended the Patuxent River to Benedict, Maryland. There it deposited a landing force of 4,000 British veterans commanded by General Robert Ross. Advancing toward Washington, Ross's veterans brushed aside a hastily gathered American army at Bladensburg and on August 24 entered the capital. Congressmen, cabinet officers, and the president were sent scurrying into the Virginia and Maryland countryside to avoid capture. Finding no one with whom to negotiate for ransom for the city, the triumphant British set fire to the public buildings and returned to their ships.

In Kentucky the partial destruction of Washington was held by some observers to be an event of little consequence to the outcome of the war. Unlike European governments, the editor of the *Kentucky Gazette* declared, "Congress can convene and transact the national business at any other place just as well as it could be done at Washington." Another writer, who signed himself "Greene," agreed. He found it strange that so many of the nation's "pavement and chimney corner generals [were] . . . so sensitive about the capture of Washington and so careless of much greater errors of the administration." Repeal of the embargo, Greene asserted, was a thousand times more disgraceful, and the loss of a single ship on Lake Ontario far more injurious, than the loss of Washington. It was even asserted by some in the state that the capture of the capital would be a fortunate event, if it ended the administration's "general hankering after and calculation on peace" and inspired a more warlike spirit in the government.

Such sentiments did not deter Kentuckians from roundly condemning Madison for his lack of foresight in neglecting the city's defenses. The president came under heaviest fire, however, as a result of Secretary of War John Armstrong's resignation in the aftermath of the Washington debacle. In sharp contrast to the argument that Washington's loss was of little consequence, many Kentuckians considered Armstrong's resignation a major blow to the American cause. One Kentucky legislator explained that the former secretary's popularity stemmed from his having been the most capable man in a cabinet "where indecision and temporising have been the order of the day." Convinced that Madison had forced Armstrong to resign, some Kentuckians speculated that he had done so to eliminate a potential rival to Secretary of State James Monroe's aspirations for the presidency in 1816. Others accused the president of succumbing to pressure from a hysterical Washington populace. "Who is President?" they queried in Kentucky newspapers, "Mr. Madison or the mob of Washington?" There were even offers to march to the District of Columbia and forcibly free Madison from the duress of Washington opinion.

The furor over Armstrong's resignation continued for months in Kentucky. According to a letter published in the *Kentucky Gazette*, Madison's action found favor only with Kentucky Federalists and with intimate friends of William Henry Harrison, who had resigned his commission after the Thames campaign rather than accept assignment by Armstrong to an inactive theater of command. Certainly the *Gazette* itself was not among those who defended Madison. Fielding Bradford, who had recently acquired ownership of the newspaper, declared that the "late act of open imbecility of Mr. Madison" made it necessary for Congress to assume the initiative in military affairs. "It should now be regarded as treason for them [Congress] to wait for the President's recommendation in any thing," he continued. "The people rely on Congress only, and not on the president."

Though dissatisfaction with Madison continued, the sense of foreboding that had pervaded the state since news of Napoleon's abdication was largely dispelled in early October by reports of significant American military successes at Baltimore and at Plattsburg, New York. Master-Commandant Thomas MacDonough's victory over a British fleet at Plattsburg Bay on September 11 left MacDonough's flotilla in undisputed command of Lake

Champlain. Bereft of naval support, a well-equipped army of 11,000 British veterans thrusting south toward New York City was forced to lift its siege of Plattsburg, abandon its invasion plans, and withdraw from American soil. Three days later the British army that had seized Washington and harassed the shores of Chesapeake Bay was turned back at Baltimore. Lexington was reported to be "the seat of illumination and joy" following the "glorious" repulse of the two invading armies. Cautious hopes were aroused in the state that the war was again turning in favor of the United States.

Few Kentuckians were encouraged to believe that the conquest of Canada was again within American reach. But the victories at Plattsburg and Baltimore did create a strong conviction that the United States should reject any British peace overtures that did not include recognition of every right due a sovereign, independent nation. There was evident concern in the state that the Anglo-American peace talks begun in August at Ghent, Belgium, would result in a treaty that sacrificed important national rights in return for an early end to the war. Despite the recent repulse of two attempted British invasions, the press and others in Kentucky insisted, peace talks were premature. Suspicions that Madison was prepared to agree to any treaty that would conclude hostilities were partly responsible for Kentuckians' concern over the outcome of the peace negotiations. The Lexington *Reporter* reviewed instructions given the American negotiators by Madison and pronounced humiliating the terms the peace commissioners were authorized to accept.

Kentuckians were equally concerned at this time about the effects growing antiwar protests in New England might have upon future American military efforts. The influence Federalist critics of the war exerted upon Madison was widely regarded in Kentucky as excessive. And the belief had long been current in the state that New England Federalists would go to any lengths to prevent the United States from achieving victory over Great Britain. Governor Shelby accurately reflected prevailing opinion in the state, when he described New England Federalists as "a faction as relentless as the fire that is unquenchable, capable of thwarting her [the United States'] best interests & whose poisoness [sic] breath is extending to every corner of the Nation."

When in October the Massachusetts legislature called upon the New England states to send delegates to a special convention at Hartford in mid-December, Kentuckians were convinced that the purpose of the meeting was to dismantle the Union. The General Assembly responded to the Massachusetts legislature's proposal by adopting resolutions reaffirming Kentucky's adherence to the Constitution and condemning antiwar New Englanders for threatening secession in a time of national crisis. In the Kentucky press the promoters of the Hartford Convention were reviled as traitors and as agents of the British.

In their vocal demands after France's defeat both for an end to antiwar protest and for a determined resistance to Great Britain, Kentuckians displayed greater unity and resolution than they had since the River Raisin massacre in January 1813. Aside from moral and financial support, however, the state's contribution to the American military effort was far less than in previous years. Enlistments for military service declined sharply in Kentucky after the American victory in the Battle of the Thames. Despite growing sentiment for a larger regular army, fewer regulars were recruited in Kentucky in 1814 than in either of the two preceding war years. The only United States army regiment recruited in the state in 1814 was a portion of the newly created Second Rifle Regiment. On the basis of the regiment's authorized strength of 106 officers and men per company, it has been estimated that enlistments in the six companies raised in Kentucky probably totaled about 500. Assuming that estimate to be accurate, Kentucky provided 4,156 troops (including regulars, militia, and volunteers) for military service in 1814. This contrasts with 11,114 in 1812 and 9,495 in 1813.

In part the decline in the number of troops furnished by Kentucky after 1813 was due to the state's distant location from the principal theaters of war. But it was also due to a widespread feeling among Kentuckians that their responsibility for direct participation in the war had come to an end with the victory at the Thames. Attorney William T. Barry's attitude toward further service in the war, and toward the war itself, typified that of many Kentuckians. "You may rest satisfied, my dear, that I shall not turn *soldier* again in any short time," Barry wrote to his wife following the Thames campaign. "The war upon our frontier, it is to be hoped is ended. . . . I have been one of the fortunate persons that contributed to the glorious struggle that is terminated."

Although the General Assembly raised taxes in Kentucky in February 1814 in response to higher federal taxes imposed upon the states by Congress, little of significance was done by the legislature to prepare the state for future military emergencies or the militia for further service. Efforts to improve the state's militia system were limited to refinements in the methods used for completing and reporting muster rolls and individual service records. The many fundamental reforms needed to make the state militia a more effective fighting force were ignored. Nor was anything done by the legislature following the 1813 campaigns in the Northwest to replenish the state's exhausted stores of militia arms and equipment.

Governor Shelby's actions also reflected a feeling that Kentucky's responsibility for further military contributions to the American war effort had ended. Through much of the year his principal energies were devoted to obtaining federal pay for volunteers who had served with him in the Thames campaign and compensation for the horses they had lost. In early July 1814 the War Department once more called upon Shelby to enlist and hold ready 5,500 militia troops to meet the threat of impending invasion, probably by way of Lake Champlain. In contrast to his vigorous exertions in earlier years to provide any troops requested, Shelby privately assured militia officers in the state that he doubted whether the force recently requested by the War Department would ever be called into active service. Although he issued the appropriate orders for raising the levy, few volunteers were obtained. The men needed to fill the quota had to be procured by draft.

Even with the aid of a draft, the new detachment of Kentucky troops was organized exceptionally slowly. It was August 12 before Shelby received a requisition from General Duncan McArthur, the commanding officer of American forces in the Northwest, for 1,000 Kentucky militiamen to strengthen the garrison at Detroit. At that time not a single regiment of the detachment ordered embodied the previous month had reported a full complement of recruits. And in any event Shelby was less than eager to honor McArthur's requisition. In a letter to the secretary of war he protested the call upon Kentucky to supply men to defend a post on the frontier of "the populous State of Ohio."

In his letter Shelby attributed Kentuckians' reluctance to serve to the federal government's delay in paying many of the volunteers who had fought in the Thames campaign. Because to do otherwise might harm the American cause, Shelby stated that he would order the troops requested by McArthur to rendezvous at Newport on the Ohio River. But he pointedly implied that he would not permit the men to leave the state until the War Department had guaranteed their pay. In view of the government's failure to pay the volunteers who had served with him in Canada, Shelby explained, it was his duty as governor "to be more cautious in complying with demands upon this state for troops; And to come to an explicit understanding with the war department upon the subject [of their pay]."

The feeling that Kentucky's responsibility for further

contributions to the American military effort had ended with the conclusion of the war in the Northwest became most apparent in the state's lethargic response to early warnings of a possible British attack on Louisiana. An urgent appeal from Louisiana Governor William C. C. Claiborne for Kentucky troops to aid in the defense of New Orleans reached Shelby in September 1814. This was followed in October by a War Department order directing Shelby to send 2,500 Kentucky militiamen to reinforce General Andrew Jackson's army in the Southwest theater. A subsequent letter received a few days later from Tennessee Governor Willie Blount politely urged Shelby to hasten the troops to the front with all due speed.

Shelby accordingly ordered three regiments of the 5,500 militiamen called up in July and August to rendezvous at separate points on the Ohio River and descend by boat to New Orleans. The War Department, however, had made no provisions for equipping, provisioning, and transporting the Kentucky reinforcements. Since the Kentucky General Assembly had failed to replenish exhausted state stores following the campaigns of 1813, Shelby was unable to make up the deficiencies in money and materiel necessary to prepare the detachment for service. Nor did the legislature, when it finally convened in December, seem inclined to act energetically to remedy the situation.

The result was that the departure of the expedition from Kentucky was long delayed and would not have been possible at all except for the individual initiative of a few private citizens. Because Shelby could locate only 254 stand of state-owned arms with which to equip the troops, the bulk of the men were required to furnish their own arms and ammunition. Many failed to do so and eventually departed for New Orleans without weapons. Meanwhile, boats to convey the men to New Orleans were provided at the personal risk of James Taylor, quartermaster of Kentucky militia. Lacking authority to requisition state funds with which to purchase boats, Taylor mortgaged his plantation for $6,000 and relied upon the War Department to reimburse him before the sixty-day note expired.

Even funds to purchase food for the troops were wanting. By early December a sufficient number of boats had been collected at Louisville to accommodate two of the regiments destined for New Orleans. The waiting flatboats stretched along the Kentucky bank of the Ohio River for two miles, but the troops could not embark for lack of provisions. A youthful resident of Louisville, David Meriwether, later recalled that "the quartermaster and commissary departments were scarce of funds which induced my father, William Pope, Matthew Love, and others to endorse a note in the old Bank of Kentucky . . . for one hundred thousand or two hundred thousand dollars which was to be applied for the purchase of provisions, etc., for the troops." When the bank refused the loan on the grounds that it had already issued paper money to the full amount permitted by its charter, young Meriwether was sent to Frankfort with messages demanding action from the Jefferson County representatives in the General Assembly. Only then did the Assembly act to authorize a further extension of bank credit for the purchase of provisions.

By January 4, 1815, when the Kentucky reinforcements called for in October finally reached New Orleans, a British army of 9,000 men under General Sir Edward Pakenham was already preparing for a decisive engagement with Jackson's army of 5,000 militiamen, regulars, and volunteers. According to Isaac Shelby, the Kentucky contingents belatedly arriving in Jackson's camp were, in large part, "composed by drafts & substitutes from amongst the poorer kind of citizens." Even convicted criminals had been permitted to enlist rather than face imprisonment.

If the quality of the Kentucky troops was, in Shelby's

opinion, lamentable, their lack of proper arms and equipment was appalling. It was reported to Shelby in November that fewer than one in thirty of the men thus far mustered for the expedition were armed. Upon their arrival at New Orleans in January, Andrew Jackson was at first incredulous that most of the Kentucky reinforcements were said to be without weapons. "I don't believe it," he reportedly exclaimed. "I have never seen a Kentuckian without a gun and a pack of cards and a bottle of whiskey in my life." But after investigating, Jackson reported to the War Department that barely a third of the Kentucky troops were armed and that the arms they had were barely fit for use. Moreover, he found the Kentuckians had been sent into the field without tents, proper bedding, cooking utensils, and many without adequate clothing. So destitute was their condition that the Louisiana legislature voted $6,000 for their immediate relief. Sympathetic citizens of New Orleans, after visiting the Kentucky camp, raised another $10,000 by public subscription; and the ladies of the city, shocked by the ragged and impoverished condition of the Kentuckians, made and distributed clothing among the men.

There was little time for further efforts on behalf of the Kentucky troops, however. Nine miles below New Orleans the British and American armies were readying themselves for battle. To oppose the British advance on the city Jackson had positioned his forces across a flat plain with the Mississippi River on his right and an impenetrable cypress swamp on his left. The American line was fronted by a ditch or canal up to four feet deep and a parapet, made partly of cotton bales, five feet high. It was a strong position that could only be breached by a direct frontal assault.

On the eve of the battle of January 8, 1815, Brigadier General John Adair succeeded to the command of the Kentucky troops, replacing Major General John Thomas who had fallen ill. Having heard of a cache of muskets stored in the city, the energetic Adair hastened to New Orleans and procured sufficient weapons to bring the total number of armed Kentuckians to approximately 1,000. These troops, with Adair in command, were ordered to place themselves in a position to support the center of Jackson's line. When Pakenham's redcoated veterans advanced against Jackson's position in the early morning of January 8, Adair's Kentuckians were moved into the firing line at the main point of attack and effectively aided in beating back the British assault. During the battle little could be seen through the dense smoke except rank after rank of British veterans pressing determinedly toward the American parapet. But as the firing ended the smoke drifted slowly away, revealing more than 2,000 British dead and wounded, including Pakenham himself, carpeting the blood-drenched field before the American line.

Meanwhile, approximately 1,200 unarmed Kentucky troops had remained under the command of Major General John Thomas. Not all of them had been idle, however. On January 7, the day before the battle, 400–500 of these troops were ordered by Jackson to reinforce General David Morgan's command of 450 Louisiana militia on the west bank of the Mississippi River opposite the main battlefield. Colonel John Davis was selected to lead the unarmed detachment. Davis's orders were to march five miles up the east side of the river to New Orleans, arm his men from a store of rifles and muskets reportedly lying in the city armory, and march five miles down the west bank of the river to his new position.

Unfortunately, the arms supposed to be stored at the city armory were the same weapons taken earlier by General Adair for the use of his troops. The result was that after scouring New Orleans through much of the night of January 7-8, Davis and his men were able to collect fewer than 200 weapons of varying descriptions, age, and usefulness. Armed with this miscellaneous and nearly useless assortment of guns, between 170 and 200 Kentuckians trudged wearily into Morgan's camp shortly before dawn on the morning of the Battle of New Orleans.

Despite their sleepless night, Davis's Kentuckians were immediately ordered to reinforce a small contingent of Louisiana militia already sent forward to slow the advance of 1,200 British troops disembarking on the west bank under Colonel William Thornton. Reaching the Louisianians about a mile below the main American line just as the British advance began, the Kentuckians found themselves facing overwhelming odds. Unable to stand, they fired one or two volleys in the direction of the advancing British and fell back upon Morgan's position. Davis was then ordered by Morgan to place his men in an open plain approximately 200 yards to the right of the main body of Louisiana troops.

It was an impossible position for Davis to defend. On their left the Kentuckians were widely separated from Morgan's main body. To their right stretched a broad plain defended only by a few pickets. As they came on the British perceived and struck hard at the gap between Morgan's Louisiana militia and Davis's Kentuckians. Thornton, at the same time, extended his line to outflank the Kentuckians on their right. Outnumbered and threatened on both flanks, Davis and his men began to fall back from their exposed position. Morgan's Louisianians, also unable to hold, began falling back as well and the retreat quickly turned into a rout.

The frontal assault against Jackson's position on the east bank of the Mississippi had already been bloodily repulsed by the time the smaller battle on the west bank began. Standing on the parapet, Jackson, Adair, and others were helpless spectators to the American defeat on the west bank. Fortunately for Jackson, the British had suffered such great losses in the assault on his lines that they were unable to follow up on Thornton's victory on the opposite side of the river. Thornton's troops were recalled, and the British opportunity to seize New Orleans was lost.

Jackson's crushing defeat of the British at New Orleans made him the most celebrated hero of the war of 1812. But his official report to the secretary of war touched off a controversy over the role of Kentucky troops at New Orleans that lasted until 1817 and contributed to John Adair's election as governor in 1820. In his report Jackson greatly underestimated the number of Kentucky troops engaged in the victory on the east bank and attributed the defeat on the west bank to the "inglorious" flight of Davis's Kentuckians. Adair and others in Kentucky were outraged by the slight to the Kentuckians who fought on the east bank and were angered by the imputation of cowardice on the part of Davis's command. As commander of Kentucky's troops during the battle, Adair sought an explanation and a retraction from Jackson. Jackson was adamant in his refusal, and for two years he and Adair exchanged heated words by letter and through the press. A court-martial that cleared Colonel Davis of any conduct deserving censure did nothing to abate the controversy. Although Jackson permitted the quarrel to die after a particularly rancorous and much publicized exchange of letters with Adair in 1817, Kentuckians for several years continued to harbor considerable animosity toward the victor of New Orleans.

The outcome of the struggle before New Orleans was not known in Kentucky for several weeks after the battle of January 8. Reports reached the state in early 1815 confirming that the British had struck in Louisiana rather than at Mobile as some had originally anticipated. By mid-January, the first clashes between Jackson's forces and the advancing British army were reported in the Kentucky press, although their outcome had not been fully ascertained. Five days before Jackson's final victory over the British was reported in the state, Shelby addressed the General Assembly on the military situation in the Southwest. Though hopeful that Jackson would be able to save New Orleans, Shelby believed that Louisiana would become a principal theater of war. Congress, he asserted in his address, could not be relied upon to carry the burden of war in the Southwest. Therefore, he recommended that the legislature authorize the organization of 10,000 militiamen to serve in Louisiana and provide adequate funds to equip and support them.

The following day, January 26, the General Assembly passed a bill complying with the governor's recommendation. The bill authorized the organization of 10,000 militiamen for up to six months' service. It also gave the governor authority to draw up to $100,000 from the state treasury and permission to borrow from the Bank of Kentucky any other monies needed to equip the troops. But the final provision in the bill negated any possibility of immediate action by making all other provisions contingent upon obtaining prior assurance for repayment for state expenditures from the federal government.

Before the bill was signed into law news arrived that the British had withdrawn from Louisiana after suffering the bloodiest defeat of the war. Newspaper accounts of the Battle of New Orleans were supplemented by even more vivid descriptions in letters from combatants. "Dear Samuel I have seen the enemy Completely scourged their loss was great," Kentucky militiaman David Weller wrote from New Orleans following the battle of January 8. Weller, whose company had been in the center of the American line, continued: "The red Coats lay thick enough to walk Clear of touched ground before our Company there was only one man kild near us and he had his Brains Shot out on me and I was as Bloody as a Butcher."

Throughout the state Kentuckians rejoiced at the news from New Orleans. At Lexington the announcement was celebrated with worship services at the town's churches in the morning, orations on the courthouse lawn in the afternoon, and fireworks displays in the evening. The

General Assembly proclaimed March 24 a day of thanksgiving for the victory, and still greater demonstrations were planned for that day. Before those plans could be acted upon, copies of the proposed treaty—signed at Ghent on Christmas Eve 1814—were published by the Kentucky press. Soon afterward the news arrived that the United States Senate, on February 15, had ratified the treaty. The war was at an end!

DISMAY, RELIEF, AND PRIDE

THE TREATY OF GHENT settled none of the issues over which the War of 1812 had presumably been fought. The questions of impressment and neutral rights were not mentioned, and other substantive questions were referred to commissions for future settlement. In essence both sides simply agreed to cease hostilities and return to their prewar territorial boundaries.

In Kentucky initial public reactions to the treaty ranged from dismay to relief. Those who were at first dismayed by the peace terms contended that the United States had failed to gain positive recognition of the fundamental national rights which Americans had fought to maintain. Failure to do so, they argued, combined with evidences during the war of administrative weakness, domestic disunity, and military ineptitude would invite future British impositions on American sovereignty. In opposition to this viewpoint, those who were relieved to see hostilities at an end asserted that the principal causes for war had ceased to exist with the restoration of peace in Europe. It was fruitless to continue fighting for the abstract principle of neutral rights, they insisted, when the practices that had given rise to the controversy had been abandoned by the former European belligerents.

Before the end of 1815, however, many of the initial uncertainties within the state regarding American gains in the War of 1812 were apparently resolved. During the latter half of the year statements pertaining to the War of 1812 indicated increasing agreement among Kentuckians that the United States had achieved substantial gains from the conflict. The successful defense of the nation against repeated British invasions, Kentuckians eventually concluded, had proven the stability of republican governments and had increased American prestige abroad. There was also growing confidence that the losses inflicted upon Great Britain during the war were sufficiently severe to insure that the British government would be wary of imposing upon American rights in the future. As it became clear that its opposition to the war had effectively crushed the Federalist party in the United States, Kentuckians found still another cause for satisfaction with the outcome of the conflict. But they remained cautious enough to insist that future security depended heavily upon increasing national economic strength, particularly through increases in domestic manufactures, and upon maintaining a larger, improved military establishment.

In this latter respect the War of 1812 had brought a turning point in Kentuckians' attitudes toward the American military system. The militia continued to be regarded as the basis of American military strength. Nevertheless, the threat of British invasion in 1814 had forced many Kentuckians to acknowledge the inadequacies of a decentralized military organization. Demands for federally imposed uniformity in the nation's militia system and for a larger peacetime military establishment stemmed from a heightened recognition that centralized authority over military affairs is a necessary attribute of national power.

If Kentuckians gradually found cause for rejoicing in the outcome of the War of 1812, they had still greater cause for pride in the part they had played in the conflict. Kentucky's military role in the War of 1812 was exemplary. It is true that enthusiasm for the war fluctuated radically in the state as the tide of battle ebbed and flowed. Considering the many reverses and disappointments encountered during the lengthy conflict, this could hardly have been avoided. It was particularly unavoidable since Kentuckians, despite widespread rejoicing in 1812 over the declaration of war, were in reality ill prepared psychologically and militarily for the conflict. Accustomed to fighting essentially local wars for local ends, few Kentuckians at the beginning of the War of 1812 foresaw the possibility of a prolonged contest on land or the advantages of regular over militia armies.

Given the same lack of experience with war on a wide scale, Kentuckians could hardly have been expected to manifest great enthusiasm for service outside the state's immediate locale. Virtually no one in Kentucky, at the beginning of the War of 1812, expected militia from any state to participate extensively in military operations outside their own region or in adjoining British territory. Common economic interests and a history of past wars against the British and Indians in the Northwest Territory caused Kentuckians to feel a greater kinship with settlers in Ohio, Indiana, and Illinois than with the people of any other section. It was taken for granted, therefore, that Kentucky's primary responsibilities in the War of 1812 would be to defend the northwestern frontier against Britain's Indian allies and to participate actively in the projected invasion of Upper Canada. It was natural that from the beginning to the end of the conflict, Kentucky militia and volunteers should exhibit a distinct preference for military service in the Northwest.

In Kentucky so strong was the concept of state responsibility for regional defense that it is doubtful whether an equal number of troops could have been raised in the state had the American Northwest not become a major theater of war. With the exception of the 2,500 state troops sent from Kentucky to New Orleans near the end of the war, no militia or volunteers recruited by Governor Shelby were requested to serve in any theater of war other than the Northwest. To a large extent, the same was true of the regular troops recruited in the state. The Nineteenth Infantry Regiment, half of which was recruited in Kentucky, participated in an unsuccessful attack upon Fort Erie in June 1814 and in a successful attack on the same post the next month. A detachment from the all-Kentucky Seventeenth Infantry also took part in the capture of Fort Erie and formed part of the garrison that repulsed a prolonged, hard-fought British siege of the fortress during August and September. With the exception of the three actions at Fort Erie on the Niagara River, all of the twenty-three separate engagements in which regular regiments recruited wholly or partially in Kentucky are known to have taken part were fought either in the Northwest or at New Orleans.

Although the state's participation in American military campaigns was thus limited largely to the Northwest and Louisiana, the high percentage of eligible Kentucky fighting men who volunteered for service in those areas affirms the sincerity of the patriotic rhetoric that characterized Kentucky oratory and journalism before and during the war. In the northwestern campaigns and at New Orleans, the exploits of numerous individual Kentuckians helped create a romantic, almost legendary, image of the Kentucky fighting man. But the state's best claim to a place of prominence in the War of 1812 lies in the number of Kentuckians who fought and died in the conflict.

The United States put forty-eight regiments of regulars of all descriptions into the field during the War of 1812. Following a practice established in 1808, recruitment of these regiments was assigned to specific states. Twenty-eight of the forty-eight regiments were recruited in the populous states of the Northeast. The southern seaboard states from Delaware through South Carolina provided another ten regiments. Although Kentucky's white population was only 324,237 in 1810, the year of the last census preceding the war, the equivalent of slightly more than four of the authorized regiments of regulars was recruited exclusively in Kentucky.

The regiments furnished by Kentucky included the Seventh, Seventeenth, and Twenty-eighth infantry regiments, each of which was recruited in its entirety in the state. Half of the Nineteenth Infantry and about two-thirds of the Second Rifle Regiment were also enlisted in Kentucky, with the remainder of the two regiments being drawn from Ohio. Altogether, about 3,800 Kentuckians enlisted in regular army units during the War of 1812, most of them for five years or the duration of the war.

By far the greater portion of the 556,622 Americans who served during the War of 1812 did so as militia or as volunteers recruited for short periods of time to participate in specific campaigns. The same was true in Kentucky. The closest approximation possible on the basis of surviving records indicates that Kentucky furnished 25,705 troops for the War of 1812, including regulars, militia, and volunteers. Of these 21,905 were either militia or volunteers. On the assumption that about one-fifth of Kentucky's white population in 1812 was male and of an age and physical condition to engage in military service, it has been estimated that between four and five of every six eligible men in the state saw some service during the War of 1812.

That so many of Kentucky's fighting men volunteered for military duty in the War of 1812 is even more remarkable when it is recalled that Kentucky was never seriously threatened by enemy invasion. Distant from the ocean and largely sheltered from British and Indian attacks by settled or partially settled states and territories, Kentucky had little need to maintain fortifications or a large home guard. The result was that while more heavily populated seaboard states like Massachusetts and Virginia raised a larger number of militia and volunteer troops than Kentucky, many of those troops were recruited for garrison duty or home defense and saw little or no action. In contrast, almost every man recruited in Kentucky was specifically enlisted for active campaigns against the British or their Indian allies.

The most impressive evidence of the major role played by Kentucky troops in the actual fighting of the War of 1812 is the high proportion of Kentuckians among the total number of Americans killed in battle. Approximately 1,200 of the 1,876 Americans killed in battle in the War of 1812 were Kentuckians. Thus, while the 25,705 regulars, militia, and volunteers that Kentucky provided represented only 4.6 percent of the troops who served in American armies during the war, 64 percent of all Americans killed in battle in the War of 1812 were Kentuckians.

Bibliographical Essay

THIS BOOK IS based largely upon research embodied in the last three chapters of the author's doctoral dissertation. Although the text has been rewritten for purposes of this publication, those readers who are interested in specific documentation for the main points included here may refer to James W. Hammack, Jr., "Kentucky and Anglo-American Relations, 1803–1815" (Ph.D. diss., University of Kentucky, 1974).

Readers with a more general interest in Kentucky's role in the War of 1812 will find numerous sources of published and unpublished information available to them. At the Kentucky Historical Society in Frankfort, The Filson Club in Louisville, and the Margaret I. King Library at the University of Kentucky many letters, journals, and newspapers from the War of 1812 period have been preserved in manuscript or microfilmed form. The most useful published and unpublished contemporary sources covering all or most of the war period are *Annals of Congress*, 42 vols. (Washington, D.C., 1834–1856); Lexington *Kentucky Gazette;* Lexington *Reporter;* James F. Hopkins, ed., *The Papers of Henry Clay*, vols. 1 and 2 (Lexington, Ky., 1959, 1961); "Isaac Shelby Letter Book 'A' " and "Isaac Shelby Letter Book 'B' " (Kentucky Historical Society, Frankfort); Kentucky General Assembly, *Journal of the House of Representatives* and *Journal of the Senate* (Frankfort, 1812–1816); and *Acts of the General Assembly of Kentucky* (Frankfort, 1812–1815).

Contemporary letters and accounts pertaining to specific campaigns or to particular phases of the War of 1812 are still more numerous. Among the many unpublished letters and journals in which particular aspects of wartime activities are described, the Allen Papers and the Isaac Shelby Papers at the Margaret I. King Library, University of Kentucky, contain valuable information. The same is true of the following collections held by The Filson Club, Louisville, Ky.: William Taylor Barry Papers, James Young Love Papers, Robert B. McAfee Papers, Samuel McDowell Papers, David Meriwether Memoirs, Preston Family Papers, Weller Family Papers.

Correspondence and more complete contemporary accounts of certain phases of the War of 1812 have in some instances been published. Those most descriptive of Kentucky's role in the War of 1812 are William Atherton, *Narrative of the Suffering and Defeat of the Northwestern Army, under General Winchester . . . .* (Frankfort, Ky., 1842); Elias Darnall, *A Journal, Containing an accurate & interesting account of the hardships, sufferings, battles, Defeat, & captivity of those heroic Kentucky Volunteers & Regulars, commanded by General Winchester, in the year 1812–1813* (Paris, Ky., 1813); Logan B. Esarey, ed., *Messages and Letters of William Henry Harrison*, 2 vols. (Indianapolis, Ind., 1922); James Taylor Eubank, "The Siege of Fort Meigs," *Register of the Kentucky Historical Society* 19 (May 1921): 54–62; William B. Northcutt, "War of 1812 Diary of William B. Northcutt," G. Glenn Clift, ed., *Register of the Kentucky Historical Society* 56 (April 1958): 165–80; (July 1958): 253–69; (October 1958): 325–43; James A. Padgett, ed., "The Letters of Colonel Richard M. Johnson of Kentucky," *Register of the Kentucky Historical Society* 38 (July 1940): 186–201; (October 1940): 323–39; and "Letters of Hubbard Taylor to President James Madison," *Register of the Kentucky Historical Society* 36 (April 1938): 95–127; (July 1938): 210–39; Samuel Stubbs, *A Compendious Account of the Late War, to Which is added, the Curious Adventures of Corporal Samuel Stubbs (a Kentuckian of 65 years of age)* (New York, 1915).

Of the several general histories of the War of 1812, the most recent is Reginald Horsman, *The War of 1812* (New York, 1969). Earlier works of a similar nature are Francis F. Beirne, *The War of 1812* (New York, 1949), and Harry L. Coles, *The War of 1812* (Chicago, 1965). Though exceptionally harsh in many of its judgments, Henry Adams's accounts of the United States during the war period in *History of the United States of America during the Administrations of Jefferson and Madison*, 9 vols., reprint ed. (New York, 1962), are still highly useful as well as vigorously written.

Two works dealing specifically with the War of 1812 in the Northwest are particularly informative for those interested in Kentucky's role in the war. They are Alec R. Gilpin, *The War of 1812 in the Old Northwest* (East Lansing, Mich., 1958), and Robert B. McAfee, *History of the Late War in the Western Country*, reprint ed. (Bowling Green, Ohio, 1919). McAfee's account is based partly upon his own careful records of campaigns in which he participated during the war.

Further information about Kentucky during the war years, the state's role in specific campaigns, and the activities of individual Kentuckians can be found in the following list of selected sources:

Barce, Elmore. "Tecumseh's Confederacy." *Indiana Magazine of History* 13: 161–74.

Beasley, Paul W. "The Life and Times of Isaac Shelby, 1750–1826." Ph.D. diss., University of Kentucky, 1968.

Brooks, Charles B. *The Siege of New Orleans*. Seattle, Wash., 1961.

Clark, Thomas D. *A History of Kentucky*. Lexington, Ky., 1960.

———. "Kentucky in the Northwest Campaign." In *After Tippecanoe: Some Aspects of the War of 1812*, edited by Philip P. Mason. East Lansing, Mich., 1963.

Cleaves, Freeman. *Old Tippecanoe: William Henry Harrison and His Time*. New York, 1939.

Clift, G. Glenn. *Remember the Raisin!* Frankfort, Ky., 1961.

Hamilton, Holman. *Zachary Taylor: Soldier of the Republic*. Indianapolis, Ind., 1941.

Hay, Robert Pettus. "A Jubilee for Freemen: The Fourth of July in Frontier Kentucky, 1788–1816." *Register of the Kentucky Historical Society* 64: 169–95.

Kerr, Charles S., ed. *History of Kentucky*. 5 vols. Chicago, 1922.

Meyer, Leland W. *The Life and Times of Colonel Richard M. Johnson of Kentucky*. New York, 1967.

Pirtle, Alfred. *The Battle of Tippecanoe*. Filson Club Publications, No. 15. Louisville, Ky., 1900.

Quaife, Milo. "Governor Shelby's Army in the River Thames Campaign," *Filson Club History Quarterly* 10: 57–65.

Roberts, Gerald F. "William O. Butler: Kentucky Cavalier." Master's thesis, University of Kentucky, 1971.

Smith, Zachary F. *The Battle of New Orleans*. Filson Club Publications, No. 19. Louisville, Ky., 1904.

Talbert, Charles G. "The Life of William Whitley." *Filson Club History Quarterly* 25: 101–21.

Wilson, Samuel M. "Kentucky's Part in the War of 1812." *Register of the Kentucky Historical Society* 60: 1–8.

Young, Bennett H. *The Battle of the Thames*. Filson Club Publications, No. 18. Louisville, Ky., 1903.